Ask Dave:

Usable Answers to Business Questions

David Conrad, Ed.D.

Heuristic Books

Chesterfield Missouri

USA

Copyright

Published, July, 2013

ISBN 9781596300842

LCCN: 2013934895

for Mathematics & Management Science
heuristicbooks.com

Heuristic Books

is an imprint of

Science & Humanities Press

PO Box 63006
Chesterfield MO 63006-7151
636-394-4950
Heuristicbooks.com

Book Dedication

To my wonderful family
of whom I could write a book of thanks.

Foreword

From working with an irate boss, or interacting with a disgruntled colleague, or even having a problem at work that needed sound and timely advice, have you ever felt that you needed a trusted advisor or confidant to provide you direct, usable solutions? The approaches to seeking work-related assistance, that we commonly adopt, range from asking our trusted friends and colleagues, to checking out Google, to searching for scholarly reviews, or even to browsing a self-help business book section at a book store. All of these sources provide great opportunities for help and learning, but may fall short in providing us what we absolutely need to know.

While asking for help from others allows us to network with friends, and reading a scholarly article builds our knowledge of the management process, these approaches, however, suffer from a few deficiencies. From being too detailed to being too diffuse, some of the advice we obtain leaves us wondering what to do next. Of course, there is always the option of doing nothing about it at all.

Professor David Conrad's book is a collection of answers to several of those thorny and sensitive questions and issues that arise at our work place. Keeping the 80/20 rule in mind — 80% of our problems arise from 20% of our colleagues and employees – it is essential to know where to look for solutions to recurring problems. Also, in a work culture where we are all expected to assemble, coach, and mentor the best teams for given challenges, we can be sure that, despite our best efforts, problems will surface. Processes, personalities, issues, and the intermingling of varying organizational cultures create a true melting pot of personalities and problems in today's work place. While each organization has its mission and vision statement, carefully-prepared organizational charts, policies, and human resource procedures to address most issues emerging at work, conflicts still happen that leave us scratching our head. Professor Conrad can help you with that itch.

Professor Conrad's book explores organizational issues and the book is written in a conversational style supplying tough questions with applicable, implementable answers. The answers are a distillation of the knowledge gained from Dr. Conrad's management experience and business education. I can say this with most certainty, because I attended Professor Conrad's classes when I was graduate business student at Augsburg College in Minnesota.

Quoting my MBA classmate, Richard Arians, "Dr. Conrad's book tells you the time and spares you the process of having to make the watch!" As I read the book, I found the answers to be based on strong evidence from business literature, where each question deals with actual business struggles (conflict management, negotiation, team-building, etc.) and the answers describe the best tactic to handle the unique situations.

The reader will also get to know a lot about Dr. Conrad's teaching philosophy from this book — Dr. Conrad hates beating around the bush. A word of advice to remember as you read the chapters: businesses deal with communications among numerous stakeholders and rely on knowledge of what is best for rapid and valid decision making, and the variation of perspectives among stakeholders results in the composition of effective teams that thrive on diversity of beliefs, perspectives, and opinions. Professor Conrad constantly reminds us to be aware of these individual differences, to be respectful of diverse views and ideas, and to get everyone on board to become decisive and unified in action and commitment.

Professor Conrad empowers us with ideas that allow us to negotiate the complex puzzles of the modern workplace. As I read this book I thought back about the situations I have been in and the answers I sought. I wish I had had Professor's Conrad's book! Well, that wish is now finally fulfilled. Readers will find a wealth of information in this book. I would recommend this book to anyone working in small or large organizations, business students, or any lifelong learners wanting to advance their workplace knowledge and skills.

Amit K. Ghosh, MD, MBA, FACP

Director of International Program,

Division of General Internal Medicine

Professor, College of Medicine

College of Medicine, Mayo Clinic

Rochester, Minnesota

Contents

Introduction

OK, here it is, a book made up of years of rants, diatribes, questionably sage wisdom, and advice from others taken from my newspaper business Q & A column titled ... drum roll, please ... "Ask Dave." Catchy, huh? Also, you can see I like to use ellipsis points. I should never have discovered them.

I'm not any smarter—nor dumber—than your average business management writer; just audacious and never did understand the words, "don't do it". However, what I found over the years, is people constantly seek advice, or at least opinions about things very fundamental and important in their lives–their jobs.

You've heard it said, "what you do is who you are"; well, I believe that to an extent. I think we do tend to migrate toward work that fits who we are and also fits our motivation levels and aptitude. Of course, believers in the "Peter Principle" will tell you there are far too many who are way over-employed and should not be doing what they are doing. Hmm ... I guess I know far too many of those folks.

But, at the end of the day, we are people and we are subject to thoughts, feelings, and emotions – we are not robots, though I have had a hard time believing that with a few people I have worked with or under over the years. I digress – I'm good at digressing. My point is we want to be treated like people and often we are not.

The workplace is a cesspool of strange interactions and business never runs like a fine Swiss watch. Our vulnerabilities, egos, frailties, and personalities tend to obstruct what should be a very uncomplicated process of building and providing things to others and working with people to do it. Why do we complicate everything? Geesh!

Our work brings us in close contact with angry customers, bosses, and coworkers. We deal with communication malfunctions, resource scarcity, long hours, and inadequate pay. We see idiots get favored and promoted. We also see managers – who claim they are transformational leaders – inept, self-serving, MIA, and DOA.

On-the-job training, college degree programs, and the highest paid consultants cannot cure the ills and ailments that beset our work environment. There are not enough of those motivational wall hangings on this planet that will compel people to always "do the right thing". There are not enough great managers and inspirational leaders who practice what they preach and preach what really should be practiced.

Now, before I am accused of being a bitter old business defeatist and curmudgeon, let me say that there are so many truly skilled, kind-hearted, rationale, and fearless individuals out there that make business a true pleasure to conduct and also make the workplace a joy to be in. I hail these people and I ask them to keep doing what they are doing—we love you!

This book is for everyone who works, has worked, or will work – I want to state this clearly because I want everyone to buy my book. Seriously, the good, the bad, and the ugly in business will get an education of some sort from reading these heartfelt reader questions and the responses from yours truly.

I don't have all of the answers; but, I do have some and I most certainly have what everybody has—an opinion about this or that. I try to use data as evidence in my responses, but you will read through any attempt of mine to appear as a scholarly researcher and really appear as someone who has some rather fixed convictions.

Please move through the various sections and reflect on people, places, and events in your lives where others—and possibly yourself—failed to measure up to what may be termed "effective" and possibly even challenge yourself to gain new skills, think before acting, listen more, and try to bring out the best in others. If what we do is who we are, then do the right things.

Chapter One: Bad Bosses

Quote of the Week:

"The true test of a man's character is when he achieves some power."

Abraham Lincoln

I'll tell you right now: this is the longest chapter in the book. Why? Over the years, I have received so many questions related to coping with bad bosses. It's like there must be a world-wide chain of "bad boss schools" producing nothing but damaging, toxic bosses.

In defense of those bosses, who are really not "toxic" and are more naive or robotic in nature, a great deal of the employee complaints may be attributed to personality conflicts, rigidity of work expectations, or the jobs that people have. It is bad leadership and the tactics used by "bosses from hell" that cause the real problems.

It's those bad leaders that use threats and punishment to stop undesired behavior; use fear tactics to get followers to toe the line; let power go to their heads; do things that are in their own best interests without considering collective interests; and create factions of "in-groups" and "out-groups," rewarding in group members not because they are top performers, but because they show loyalty or fawn over the leader.

Let's take a look at some "bad leadership" struggles and, again, you can determine if my responses say something and if my advice is usable. Of course, I think it does and is ... so there!

Dear Dave,

I have a boss who shows no respect whatsoever to me and my coworkers. He even ridicules people out loud and makes them feel like crap. I have been able to avoid his poor treatment, but I can see how it is hurting my coworkers. Nobody feels good about themselves and their work. How can I help my fellow workers survive all this?

Dear T,

I hear you. I once had a boss, who thought it was good management to belittle my sales reps in front of me and others for even small errors. You could see it in their eyes that they were not only hurt and embarrassed, they also wanted to tear my boss apart. Self-esteem is that powerful.

My first thought is that the biggest self-esteem issue is that of your boss – he doesn't feel good about himself, so the only way he can compensate for this inadequacy is tormenting others. This is so sad. Don't get me wrong: I am not trying to make excuses for your boss; I am only trying to figure out what is in his pea brain.

Psychologists will tell you that poor self-esteem is one of the largest causes of destructive behavior. When we have poor self-esteem, we lack pride, well-being, and peace, so we lash out at others who may possess self-esteem, or are easy targets – we are jealous and bitter.

What is Self-Esteem?

Self-esteem is the experience of being competent to cope with the basic challenges of life and of being worthy of happiness. It is confidence in our ability to think. It is also confidence in our ability to learn, make appropriate choices and decisions, and handle change.

Organizations today need a higher level of interdependence, self-reliance, self-trust, and the capacity to exercise initiative ... in a word, self-esteem.

Building Self-Esteem in Others

Our minds are very good at picking up all the things we've done wrong, and makes sure we are aware of them. With such a counter-productive force at work, we can benefit greatly by regularly working towards establishing and building our own self-image.

As a leader, you are, whether you like it or not, a role model. The higher your self-esteem, the more likely it is you'll be able inspire the best in others. People look to others for strength and they will look to you.

Do this: try to help somebody or teach them something. Also, help them see the difference between facts and feelings – if these attacks are just vicious and unwarranted, help people see these attacks for what they are.

Cheer people up—see what you can do to make others feel good or trigger them to smile. Maybe giving them a genuine compliment, helping them with something, or telling them what you admire about them may be enough to make people gain some self-esteem.

Remember that appreciation, praise, gratitude, and recognition are some of the most powerful tools you can use to strengthen the self-esteem of others. But, be sincere when dealing out compliments, or you may appear phony.

Finally, remind your coworkers that your boss is incompetent and to not take his rants and diatribes to heart. Teach them to actually realize it is your boss who is the loser, not you folks. Also, if things are that bad and people are crumbling, tell them to do what the Amityville house told the Lutz family, "Get out!"

Dear Dave,

I left a company about 4 months ago, because the company was struggling and because I really wasn't going anywhere. The management did treat the employees well. The company I am with now has a better footing financially, but my manager is pretty abusive, except to his favorites—I am not one. My colleagues call him the "Toxic Manager." That certainly fits. How can I cope with this manager, because I am stressed-out every day?

R

Dear R,

Toxic managers are a fact of life. Some managers are toxic most of the time and most are toxic some of the time. Knowing how to deal with them is crucial to your well-being and there are coping mechanisms.

One management writer believes there are 4 types of toxic managers: narcissistic, aggressive, rigid, and impaired. He believes that underneath these difficult behaviors are personality flaws, mood disorders or impulsivity. I personally believe these folks have poor self-esteem and take it out on others – especially those who appear to have good self-esteem.

Types and Handling

Grandiose, arrogant, aloof managers tend to be masking inadequacies and low self-regard. They are critical, controlling, and easily enraged. They overcompensate for their shortcomings by acting abusively superior and even relish making peoples' lives difficult. How sad is that? But, that is the narcissistic manager.

Dealing with the narcissistic manager requires skill and tact. Don't criticize them and have a showdown. Don't admire them, but show respect. And, let them think new ideas are theirs. Seek out a mentor and build allies with your coworkers. Document your work and do not play-down your accomplishments. And, don't take all this personally. Remain proud. If push comes to shove, try to transfer...or get out.

Aggressive managers are people who have been taught it's a dog-eat-dog world and you need to step on people when you can, some twice. They are overly-competitive and they are bullies who thrive on intimidating others. They are frantic, irritable, and distressed. As I write this, I cringe.

Dealing with aggressive managers requires calm, patience, and never letting them think you are intimidated. You need to develop a thick skin and let the attacks roll off your back. I know...it's tough to do this, but taking the high road is the best and you will feel better for doing so. Also, find out what disturbs them and avoid pushing their buttons. Believe it or not, sometimes you may be able to reach them and help them see that what they are doing will lead them to greater problems.

Rigid managers have a PhD in "Controlfreakius." They have one rule: Everything must be done their way. They try so hard to avoid making mistakes and this dominates their decision-making and their life. They believe they are always being threatened and pushing back is protectionism. They love order and hierarchies. Changes just kill them and creativity (new ideas) are seen as disturbances and challenges to their autonomy and control. I believe they suffer from what I call "Organizational OCD."

Dealing with the rigidly toxic manager requires firearms – just kidding! You must not confront them and argue with them. You may be able to persuasively show them with facts and data that an idea, concept, or method is working for others and may work for the team or department. Possibly show them that somebody in authority – that they respect – is doing something this way. Always invite them into anything going on and get their participation. It's best to show how your ideas fit into their plans. What a concept!

The impaired manager is just plain nuts, or is suffering from anxiety, depression, substance abuse, or burnout. They are easily distracted, disorganized, and talk and interrupt all the time. They are fearful, withdrawn, pessimistic, and agitated. I feel bad for these managers, because their toxicity is less of a choice as are the other types. They need help and quick. In short, get them treatment. Get them treatment. And get them treatment.

You need to beef up your emotional intelligence as best you can to control your emotions and build relationships that will help you cope and grow. Seek to deal with these managers, thinking about ways to handle the situations. Then, think about the toxicity and your actions, learn from them, and do not become a toxic manager yourself.

Dear Dave,

We have a boss who drives all of us nuts. He micromanages everyone to death, I am just about finished with my college degree and I know I will soon have opportunities to find a new job. How can I cope in the meantime without losing it?

Miss Managed

Dear Miss,

Bad bosses, control freaks, jerks, micromanagers, or bumbling fools can be found in all organizations. Unfortunately, with all of the staffing cuts we have seen, there are probably more overworked and undertrained bosses than ever.

Management author, Harvey Hornstein, surveyed 1,000 employees and found that 90% of them have been subjected to abusive behavior.

So, what can you do? Sometimes the only solution is getting out. Try these tips:

Make sure you are doing everything right – this will keep you out of trouble and provide positive reinforcement for doing your job to the best of your abilities.

Compile a list of bad boss behaviors — this should be a cathartic experience for you and help you deal with the things that your boss does that drives you nuts.

Find a mentor with the company — in coping with a bad boss, a mentor can be a good sounding board for you, and help build your skills.

Don't sacrifice your health or self-esteem — stay involved, exercise, eat healthy, and maintain a vibrant life outside of work.

Do: The best job you can and act professional at all times.

Don't: Whine, complain, and suck the energy out of others.

Dear Dave,

I work at a restaurant. It seems like the owners feel their employees are dispensable and we are just something that can be used and thrown away. We are even told things like, "If you don't like it, leave" or even "You should just be lucky you got a job!" I know it is difficult to find a job, but I don't think managers should threaten us that we are instantly replaceable.

P

Dear P,

Your employer should treat employees as if they're part of the team for the long term, because they are the face of the restaurant. Rather than having a replacement mentality, your bosses need a more collaborative, respectful, and strategic approach to developing and retaining their most precious resource, their people.

Mistreatment "Ripple Effect"

Disgruntled, fearful, and stressed-out employees often wear their emotions on their sleeve and it becomes obvious to customers, too. In that vein, it makes good economic sense for managers to treat employees with compassion, kindness, and encouragement.

Evidence has shown a high correlation between employee job satisfaction and engagement, and employee retention and recruitment. In addition, nobody likes to work for a place where his or her input is not sought, or is ignored.

Sadly, there are many smart people with an unfortunate commitment to both underpaying and mistreating their employees. Making every employee within the organization exhausted and clueless as to their role and future will likely be the undoing of the company.

A Whole New Thinking

Achieving success through people means fundamentally altering the way managers think about the workforce and employee relationships. In this period of economic challenges, companies are asking more and more from their employees. That's OK, as long as the employees feel they are treated fairly and with respect.

One sales manager I know believes in the importance of companies valuing their employees. He states, "Satisfied customers start with satisfied employees. Management by threat can provide short-term compliance at the expense of long-term commitment. This was referred to in a seminar I recently attended as "managing without a license," where managers create a fear culture and not one where the employee is gaining work satisfaction."

No matter what economic conditions exist, an organization's employees—how they think and work—remain a crucial differentiating and competitive factor. While the culture and management practices that drive an effective workforce are not readily visible to outsiders, these factors can be as important as a company's products, reputation, or marketing practices.

By implementing management practices that place real value on their employees, companies can achieve competitive advantage. Those that foster an atmosphere of commitment and mutual trust will get the most from their people. On the other hand, organizations that regard their employees as dispensable are unlikely to garner their commitment, loyalty, or willingness to expend extra effort for the organization's benefit.

The True Costs

Loyalty cannot be taken for granted. According to one survey, over half of the employees queried said they expect to leave their organizations voluntarily within 2 – 3 years. What is lost with every person who leaves is valuable, including customer and business knowledge.

Plus, the open and hidden costs are great including a reduction in operational efficiency and customer service levels; loss of intimate knowledge of the customer; cost of recruitment and selection; position coverage and the manager's time; cost of induction and training; plus the decreased morale of those who remain.

Employees wonder

Employee contentment and engagement are revealed when they ask themselves these questions:

Am I rewarded fairly?

Is there an investment in training and developing me?

Does management listen to my ideas?

Does the company allow me the flexibility and give me authority to solve customer issues?

Do managers respect me as an individual?

In addition, motivating employees goes beyond incentives such as pay and working conditions. Research reveals that employees are more likely to move on if they believe they are not being treated well and given respect. To foster long term, sustained motivation, organizations must inspire employees to draw their motivation from inside, rather than rely on external factors such as pay.

In summary, employees crave managers that provide strong, positive leadership that they can trust, while attending to the growth and satisfaction of good people trying hard to contribute.

Dear Dave,

I have recently been promoted to manager of my department at a large organization. My former boss now works under me. However, he is struggling with the fact that he is not in charge. He frequently comes to my office providing unsolicited advice. I try to be polite, because I don't want to hurt his feelings, yet he is getting on my nerves. How do I deal with this situation?

Dear R,

Your former boss is suffering from separation anxiety (can't let go) and probably means well. You may be fortunate that he does try to help, rather than carry a grudge that you have taken the reins and are in control, which could lead to behind-the-scenes back-stabbing and sabotage in an effort to have you fail.

His Position

I believe your former boss believes he can help you, but he is also experiencing a personal discomfort about letting go of his past role when he was in charge. In short, he is trying to regain his ground and trying to get you to run things and give you advice the way he did when you were his employee.

There are many other reasons of why he can't let go. First, he needs to be needed and is motivated by the fact he may have a lot of knowledge in certain areas that pertain to your current situation, and needs to share it with you in order to feel wanted and important.

He may also feel helpless and less effective. He may want to help you by trying to solve your problems as a way to help. This is a strange situation for him, too, and he is trying to cope with a loss of sorts. Thus, he is overcompensating for this loss by trying to help too much.

You need to remember that he really does *not* want you to compromise your professional responsibilities and wants you to succeed. He just cannot grasp the new relationship and it will take time for him to see you can lead and handle things on your own.

For You

First, treat him the same way you treat everyone else. It is his responsibility, as much as yours, to make sure there is never the appearance that you manage certain people any differently than you manage the rest of the team. Also, treat him with respect and listen. Your consistency in showing you are a capable leader will slowly sink in

One of my colleagues always reminds me that you can't manage someone else's feelings. Instead, focus on doing the best job you can and making your team successful and productive. If, despite your best efforts, your former boss is actually disruptive to that success, then set the "sensed need of friendship" aside and let your management skills take over: setting goals, planning, delegating work, and motivating your people.

In addition, draw a boundary with him to eventually prevent loads of unsolicited advice from him. Try saying, "That's a good idea, but I have my own way of handling this," and change the subject. If he persists, tell him, "I'm glad that works for you and I know there are so many different ways of doing things, but I'm doing fine for now."

If the unsolicited advice keeps occurring, you can choose to keep ignoring it, or you can tell him, "Thanks, but I should be OK; I'm already researching a solution that I want to try, but if I need advice, I'll be sure to ask you for it."

I think you should also try to involve him in what you are planning to do and give him "special" reasonable assignments that tap into his skills and thinking. Encourage him to get others involved to get their feedback and see what they have to say. It will make him feel appreciated, and will allow you to take a directive position.

In addition, you can gently but firmly tell him that you need to try and learn things to a great extent on your own, because that is the way you learn and what works best in a lot of cases. Mention that this may even involve making a few mistakes. But, thank him for the willingness to help.

Last, but not least, create venues where all of people can offer ideas and input, but make it clear that ideas will be looked at objectively for merit and as many people as possible will be assessing the ideas for feasibility and potential value. And this includes your former boss.

Dear Dave,

A close coworker of mine just became a manager in our department. I never thought it would happen, but now she is the bossiest person I have ever seen. I never thought the promotion would go to her head, but it did. We are not as close as we used to be and in many ways I am treated like someone she has never known on a personal level. What is going on?

T

Dear T,

What's going on is this person is unprepared for the new role and is unsure how to act, so she has decided to become a dictatorial supervisor, rather than a manager and certainly not a leader.

Being promoted to management does not always come with a training manual. Unfortunately, people become managers and they haven't the foggiest what to do or how to treat people. In some ways I blame your company for letting this happen – but, maybe your company likes their managers to be cold and bossy.

Could Be Ego

On the other side of the coin, it could be your new boss likes being the way she is and this "toxic boss demon" has been lying dormant within her for several years. This means there is much that will need to take place before she gets "her leadership legs" and understands how to treat people – especially past coworkers.

Abraham Lincoln said "The greatest test of a man's character is when he achieves some power." It is possible this power trip your new manager is on is fulfilling some need she has. She may have low self-esteem and this is a way for her to over-compensate for her feelings of inadequacy. I sound like a psychologist, eh?

Your Coping Skills

You have choices on how you may wish to handle this. Here are some suggestions:

Just do your job – Stay busy, be productive, and be positive. If she is looking for someone to pounce on, don't be that person. You two may get along best if she sees you as someone who is effective and she doesn't need to worry about micro-managing the pejeepers out of you.

Confront her –Be careful, but ask her if you two can sit down, have some coffee, and talk. When you meet, kindly, gently, and sincerely ask her how you can help her in her new role and ask her what she is experiencing. She may either tell you to shut up and suck it up, or confide in you in some way about her role, challenges, and feelings.

Complain to her superiors – This is risky, because you never know what can of worms you may be opening, but if you love your work and if your boss cannot and will not change, take your case to superiors. Your argument must be based on the fact a toxic environment has emerged threatening your and others' well-being and productivity.

Get out! – If you find you cannot stay in your role and have this person as a boss, then it is time to move on. The economy is tough and jobs are not plentiful, but life is too short to work for Neanderthals with the warmth and people skills of Dr. Josef Mengele.

If this person is basically a good person, I believe she will come around in time. Give her the benefit of the doubt and just talk to her to see how you can help. Maybe that's all she really needs.

Dear Dave,

Our manager is never around and we are always covering up for him. So far, the managers above him have not become aware of his constant absence or his lack of leadership, because we are doing such a good job of making sure he does not look bad. This isn't fair and we can't do this forever. We need a good manager who is around and helps us. What do you suggest?

K

Dear K,

I understand your problem. On one hand, you fear that if you just let your manager fail, you may get dragged down with him, and on the other hand, you are sick and tired of coddling this guy and protecting his inept and careless ways.

17

Accordingly, I say, "Let him self-destruct!" However, document everything you folks are doing to work effectively despite this abomination of leadership, and keep working hard and staying positive, and let the chips fall where they may.

MIA (missing in action) Managers

Over the years I, too, have worked with and under managers who just had a careless disregard for their work and their employees. They always seemed to have little pet projects – most of which were outside of the company – and they spent their time either playing or working on the wrong things.

An "incompetent" leader by definition is someone whose actions and attitudes are either messed up and destructive, or they just are not doing anything of importance. These same leaders tend to have ingenious ways of staying below the radar and sometimes even get noticed and promoted.

MIA managers are good at getting good, well-intentioned, and hard-working individuals such as yourselves working their tails off and covering up for their disregard for both their company and their employees. Further, they have mastered the technique of being at the right place at the right time saying the right things, and taking credit.

You would think that organizations these days are focusing on getting rid of every single under-performing employee – managers included. Wrong! Unfortunately, in many cases, it is the good, high-performing employees who are shown the door, while ineffective managers – the ones who should take a hike – remain.

How You Can Cope

The sad reality is most "incompetent" leaders do not get fired; they just move on and reinvent themselves in new companies – or, if the company is large enough – they just move onto other departments and start the whole painful process of incompetence all over again.

I suggest you do two things: first, stay busy, productive, and positive — you do not want to be labeled as an incompetent employee under an incompetent boss. Second, you can document everything you see and know about this management fiasco and go to upper management telling them how this situation is hurting your productivity and your psychological well-being.

Your company's upper management are not dumb (at least not brain dead) and will, or have already noticed, your manager's incompetence and work neglect. This means that sooner or later even the slickest management incompetents will get caught and either terminated or reformed ... if possible.

Unfortunately, you will face incompetent management again – they're everywhere. However if you manage to stay calm and think about the lessons you've learned, and how to counteract incompetent behavior, you will have all the wisdom needed in order to become a better leader yourself in future jobs.

Dear Dave,

As you know, management always expects duties to be accomplished by their employees. Right? Then, why is it that management often seems to lack the ability to follow up and follow through with all their brilliant ideas? These ideas always seem to have fancy names and sound good, but what good are they if the people that come up with them don't use and support them?

A

Dear A,

Yup. You nailed it. Good ideas are only as good as the commitment behind them. An idea without legs is like a car without wheels. I like that one!

The key to success is having the motivation to follow through with your ideas and put them into action; to set goals and actively work towards achieving them.

Management Follow Through

I have always said that managers should be committed – and a few I worked for should be committed, locked up, and the key should be thrown away.

I always ask my students if they are positive they want to become a manager, because it is a tough role and especially middle management where a manager seems to get stuck and have to deal with problems, communication, and requirements coming from both up and down.

Problems occur when well-intentioned managers come up with ideas to do something or improve something and they are stuck and sidetracked by the plethora of other things they need to do or things that suddenly come up.

This is when the art and skill of delegating tasks to staff members is a necessity if they want to maintain their – and your—sanity and keep things running smoothly. However, managers must make sure employees are "ready" for delegation, so they have a fighting chance of being successful.

Also, managers need to stay on top of the tasks they delegate to ensure standards are being met. In short, telling an employee to complete a task is not enough. Managers need to follow up on the tasks that they assign to be sure the tasks are getting done correctly.

How Things Get Done

I am sure that managers do not throw out this idea or that with the intention of confusing employees or frustrating them with "flavor of the month" initiatives that will go nowhere. Managers have only so much time and running meetings (which are often unproductive - that is another topic), hiring and training staff, designing work, and many other things demand much of their time.

You could say, "Well, they just don't manage their time – that's the problem!" But, it's not that simple; they run out of time because of shifting priorities, fires that must be put out, and their constant need to monitor and control the work being done.

My belief is that employees that have proven themselves to be reliable and capable should be brought into the fold and they should be empowered to help take ideas to implementable reality. However, this assumes that a given manager can trust the employees to get to work and "let go" of the need to micromanage every little detail and piece of work.

In Summary

The name of the game for all companies and organizations these days is innovation, efficiency, change, and effectiveness. Achieving follow-through isn't difficult.

By creating an organizational culture that is aware of the benefits of delegating work and empowering good employees to complete the work, a company will see benefits and employees will not feel like they are victims of "an idea to nowhere drive-by shooting."

Dear Dave,

At my company we just do not get the help we need from our manager. I'm not sure what she is doing, but we never see her and if we do have problems or questions, we cannot find her. My friends tell me I have it good, because their bosses are always breathing down their necks and micromanaging them to death. How can we get more help from our manager?

S

Dear S,

You are not alone—in many workplaces, there is a shocking and profound lack of daily guidance, direction, feedback, and support for staff from those who are their immediate supervisors.

Too many leaders, managers, and supervisors simply do not spend enough time attending to the basics of managing staff. This is what I call "under-management" — the opposite of micro-management.

Under-management prevents employees from having have positive experiences in the workplace and get more of what they need and want. In turn, it causes managers to struggle and suffer and deliver suboptimal results.

Some management writers believe under-management is an epidemic in today's workplace. I can tell you this: most organizational problems could be avoided altogether or solved quickly by a highly-engaged, hands-on manager, who accepts his or her responsibility.

Unfortunately, highly-engaged managers are often hard to find and the ones who may choose to become more effective managers struggle to become better, because the company does not train them properly, or they want their managers to be either hands-off or absolute micro-managing Neanderthals..

Management Amuck

The signs of inadequate management are easy to spot: Staff members are confused about their roles and responsibilities, there is a general lack of planning, budgets are in chaos, and basically, nothing much is getting done.

The key here isn't just management, it's responsibility. Whether you have a decentralized organization or a strict management hierarchy, someone has to be responsible for each part of the business needs and goals – can you say management?

Part of the problem is that all too often, people are promoted to management positions not because if their people skills, but because of their competency in one area or another. Consequently, they fail to lead or manage effectively.

I think what people want from work is personal growth and an opportunity to contribute. I also think it can't just be about productivity; a manager can and should be a coach, a mentor, or a sounding board. Accordingly, a manager must very hands on (in the trenches) in a way that helps people grow – not just be better workers.

Managing Your Boss

One of my management professor colleagues tells me, if your boss won't manage you, you need to manage your boss. Successfully managing a MIA manager is a challenge but often feasible. First, you should try to understand the reasons for your boss' absent behavior. It could be anything from incompetence to a lack of motivation.

Second, you have to manage your own negative emotions regarding his/her behavior so that you do not engage in self-defeating behavior (slowing down work, or counter-attacking your boss).

Third, once you understand and have managed your own negative reactions, you can then communicate your issues/concerns—but framed in a helpful positive manner—creating an atmosphere for problem resolution.

Simply, talk to your boss and explain how people are floundering and productivity may be lost – managers hate lost productivity.

Dear Dave,

Way too many managers have what I call: A bad case of status attitude. They believe that everyone just owes them respect because they are the manager. In my book, respect must be earned in humble, professional, and ethical ways. With over 30 years with the company, I know that there are a few hot-shots that would love to walk me out the door, so I must be very careful. How come managers like mine just don't get it that respect is earned and not automatic?

No Respect

Dear NR,

What a great question, but – as you already have stated – you must be careful. The managers you refer to will not like your well-intentioned confrontations, because they will get extremely defensive and then not consider your point, only the fact that you made it and they don't like it.

Unfortunately, managers are not born with management skills and I won't even get into leadership skills. Many managers don't take the time to build rapport with their employees. Yet, results are expected quickly and little things like relationship-building sometimes gets side-stepped in the process. Other reasons include not knowing how to communicate with staff, delegate responsibly, or allow joint decision-making.

One of my MBA students explained her theory, which is many managers have self-esteem issues and just, plain don't trust themselves, so how could they possibly trust others? I agree and I also believe some managers don't have the personality, Emotional Intelligence, or the attitude to manage. Management is a people business...duh!

The reality is that today's employees have clear expectations of what they want from their leadership. And, if they get what they need, they'll respect them. Here's some management 101:

Show employees the big picture — employees want to contribute in a positive way to the organization's goals and they want to see how their work fits into the whole.

Show an interest in employee development – studies show on-the-job learning keeps a person interested in their job and helps them stay focused and committed.

Hold everyone accountable — one of the fastest ways to destroy morale and the employee's will to do more is to allow the slackers to slack... or worse... get rewarded.

24

Get into the trenches once in awhile—I often hear employees complain that their manager does not know what they do, or help do it when needed.

Be human—in today's complex world, we must recognize that employees have a life outside of work.

All of us want to be respected. We want people to believe what we say—to trust us. Trust breeds respect!

Chapter Two: Hiring

If you want to prevent organizational problems in the first place, hire the best people you can find! They may cost more, but poor performing, toxic hires will end up costing you even more.

Why is it that with the zillions of books available on the subject of hiring, the legions of trainers and consultants out there teaching hiring skills, and – especially – because of the critical need to select people carefully that we still do such a lousy job of picking the right people?

Hiring good employees is not only important to business, it is essential. Employees are the heart and soul of a business; they are the mechanism that makes a business run; they are the breath of life that enables a business to be something more than an idea or a mission statement. A business cannot run unless someone is doing the work and doing it effectively. Any intelligent business owner or manager should want good employees.

Over the years, I hired many people, and I dare say I was not a behavioral scientist nor a perfect skills matcher when hiring … I was like many other managers … I hired the people I liked and the ones I felt I really could work well with.

I was lucky and hired some gems. However, a few names and faces come to mind that were catastrophic hires and even now make me cringe, almost angry, that I was so blind and stupid in not checking these folks out more closely. Sometimes referrals are not cracked up to what they are supposed to be.

26

As a job hunter, do research: before you take a job in a new company – or even a new department – take a look at the people who work there. See if you can find out what they are like; determine if they can be trusted; try to find out if they are committed workers; and also, try to discover how they talk about and to each other. The most important hiring decision you will make is where you choose to be hired.

Managers must understand the impact of not hiring the right people. Bad employees not only affect an employer by driving down sales, costing the company unwanted expenses due to negligence or ineptness, they may even drive away that crucial stakeholder, your customers.

Let's take a look at some hiring questions and you can determine if I now make sense with my responses. You know what they say about hindsight … .

Dear Dave,

I am writing to you about an obvious workplace problem at our company – incompetent employees. Our management keeps hiring people that have few job skills and many have absolutely no people skills. This makes it very difficult for us committed and skilled employees to get our work done. Advice?

R

Dear R,

The question that must be asked in these situations is whether or not management has made a mistake in evaluating the skill level of these underperforming employees or, perhaps, whether the performance deficit is rooted in a lack of motivation and commitment to the job.

Competence and motivation must go hand-in-hand. One management consultant I know tells me that motivating an incompetent employee is like trying to teach ballet to a pig.

An article from FabJob.com titled, "Why bad employees don't get fired" identifies some common reasons poor performers are hired or kept:

1. The employee has a relationship with someone higher up—the bad employee may not perform well on the job, but may be a drinking buddy for your boss, or may simply be someone that management enjoys having around the office.

2. The boss relies on the employee—when a manager depends on an employee, the manager is less likely to attribute poor performance to the employee's ability or attitude, and more likely to attribute the poor performance to forces beyond the employee's control.

3. The employee brings more value to the company than he or she costs – in short, the employee manages to stay within the realm of what may be considered "employable."

4. The boss thinks it could be worse—even if everyone knows the employee is not pulling his or her weight, management may fear that a replacement could do an even worse job.

5. The boss is afraid of the employee—plain and simple, the boss is intimidated.

Management Musts

If the performance problems are due to incompetence, then managers must provide further training to the employees, to raise his or her skill levels to what is required to do the job. However, if an employee is the wrong fit for what is needed, and not likely to pick up the necessary skills, it is best in everyone's interest to let the employee go.

A person's lack of key skills in one work environment doesn't mean that they could not be valuable in another— possibly where the skills more appropriately complement the work that needs to be done.

In the same vein, though, just shuffling an incompetent employee around the company is insanity, especially if the reason for doing so is nobody wants to take responsibility and terminate the employee. I have seen this employee shuffle dilemma played-out in many companies.

It gets back to the logic that if you want high-performing employees, you must hire the best people you can find. They will add more value than cost.

For You

The first step in dealing with incompetent coworkers is recognizing that—while you can't change the incompetent coworkers—you *can* change your reaction to them.

Changing your reaction to a coworker's inept behavior can be accomplished by asking yourself the following questions: Is this person's lack of competence worth getting upset over? Is this person's incompetence really detrimental to me/us and how? Is this person's incompetence truly affecting me, or am I just letting it affect me?

If you have done what you can to cope with the incompetent workers, take notes and define the issues and the impact on performance, not as interpersonal problems, but as issues affecting your productivity, the work, and your progress on projects. Then, set a meeting with your boss and explain exactly what is happening.

Dear Dave,

I have a question regarding interviewing job candidates. We have so few openings and we really want the best people. Everybody I talk to hates the interview process and believes it really doesn't help you know what you need to know about the people applying for a job and I'm not sure if interviews help job candidates really understand the job and the company, either. Not only that, at our company everyone is using different ways of interviewing people and different ways of determining who to hire. Do you have any ideas about how to hire the right people?

Interview Impaired

Dear Impaired,

Your dilemma is not uncommon for companies throughout the region and nation. With the economy the way it is, there are many qualified and less than qualified individuals seeking employment, and it is crucial to have the best screening techniques in place that will match the right people to the right jobs. Also, interviews are about the best thing we have to find out things about job candidates. They are relatively quick ways for a manager to get to know important things about people.

A couple of years ago, even fast food firms were so desperate for workers that they offered up to $10 an hour for counter service work, but now there are skilled people who cannot even get interviews for positions that pay that much and are also the same jobs they would have turned their nose to a short time ago.

Thus, it is a "buyers' market" and hiring organizations can be extremely picky in their selection desires. The problem that arises in this electronic resume submission day and age is companies will be inundated with resumes and requests for interviews. Their job becomes even more difficult due to the need to screen out the undesirable candidates while not overlooking the highly qualified candidates.

I would encourage your company to develop a set of questions that are common and used by all of your interviewers to develop a consistency in inquiry. These questions should be designed to assess general organizational and interpersonal skill competencies and screen people for further consideration such as using computer technology, the ability to work in teams, communication skills, coping with ambiguity, commitment to tasks, and relationship building and leadership. Some questions can then be added that are unique to the open position and assess the basic and finite competencies that were notated as necessary candidate qualifications.

Next, I would create a question format that will more closely identify the candidates' background and experience in relation to the specific skill needs and expected qualifications of the job. This series of questions carefully matches the candidate to the position. For instance, if website design abilities are a key responsibility in the position, then directly ask for evidence of proficiency and experience in this discipline and what specific skills are possessed.

Interviewing has slowly shifted from traditional interviewing to what is now termed behavioral interviewing. Traditional interviewing is an approach that sets up a dilemma or situation and asks the interviewee to respond with what they would do to handle the situation and explain why they would handle it in that way. For example, a traditional interview question is, "If you were faced with an angry customer, what would you say and do to handle the situation?"

In contrast, behavioral interviewing seeks to find what people have actually done in real situations they have encountered. Behavioral interviewing asks the interviewee to reflect and describe a situation, challenge, or dilemma they have faced; describe the actions they took to remedy the situation; and then to explain the results of their actions.

Rarely does an interview get to be a real conversation that allows the interviewer get to know the job candidate. What if the interviewer just closed the notebook and asked some questions like: Tell me about your job dreams and nightmares. What do you laugh at? Tell me about a boss from hell. When did you really mess up? I like this one: When you pick friends, what do you look for?

In any case, the challenge for you is finding the best candidate that fits the position. Drawing out their education, skills, knowledge, and experience is the only way to determine this fit. Also, don't forget, you must be very careful to create questions that will discover if the person has the personality, ethical beliefs, and attitude that will best fit the culture, strategy, skill needs, and mission of the organization.

Finally, please, please, let the interviewee answer the questions fully and completely and do not dominate the interview. I, personally, have been in far too many interviews where the interviewer talked so much I thought I was interviewing them for a job. I learned all about them – which is important – but I felt they learned little about me.

Dear Dave,

My manager has selected a fairly new person in the department for a very desirable, newly-created supervisor position without posting the job and giving us a chance to apply. There are several of us in the department who are very qualified and would have applied. The person selected has good qualities, but lacks the experience and know-how many of us have. We have also heard this person is a friend of the son of the vice president of our company. Maybe I am venting, but is there anything we can do to protest this decision?

L,

Dear L,

Yes, there are things you can do, but you mention something very interesting and something that implies you may be hammering on cold iron … the newly-selected supervisor has a friendship with the son of a senior executive of the company—this means you need to be very careful.

Even though this appointment is grossly unfair, how you handle this – if you decide to proceed with a grievance – is important to your future with the company and how you will be viewed by upper management.

However, we know that these types of job appointments happen all the time and those who have been good, hard-working employees are simply given the shaft by being totally ignored. This amazes me when we know that companies are fighting to survive these days and throwing the dice by promoting questionably-qualified people is pure lunacy.

Not Illegal, Just Stupid

Hiring unqualified and inexperienced employees is sheer "organizational stupidity", but promoting these same people is pure "organizational insanity." Toying with the well-being of valuable, dedicated employees is idiotic.

Most employees these days are thankful, hard-working individuals who give it all for their company. Often, these people are struggling to balance their work and family lives by working long hours. In addition, many of these workers are taking college and professional classes to better themselves and to put themselves in a position to be promoted.

Accordingly, I am putting a "call out" to all managers who promote based on favoritism, nepotism, or because of stupid thinking and urging them to pull their head out … . Why a manager would risk the livelihood of the company, their own job well-being, and the culture of the company is both destructive and nuts!

Your Alternatives

First, you can say and do nothing and just suck it up. Second, you could just say, "I'm outa here" and look for other work. Or, you could take action and file a grievance. Choose wisely, my weed-hopper; you might be playing with fire and stand the chance you will be singled out as "that darn agitating troublemaker."

If you proceed to protest this decision, you must show strength in numbers and your argument must be non-emotional. Your grievance must be founded on the fact that, not only is this a violation of the well-being of all employees, but it could hamper the effectiveness of the organization.

Research what needs to be done within your company to handle such a grievance. If your company has no grievance process, this is a clear sign they not only abhor such grievance practices, but they discourage them, too.

As a group, document your thinking, rationale, and argument in a non-threatening fashion and ask for a meeting with the level of command that will be receptive to – or at least hear – your case. Remember, your grievance must be based on your concern for the company and not on how you feel. Good luck.

Dear Dave:

We hire good employees, but we have hired some really bad managers. The managers often look so good on paper and interview well, then turn out to be a bad fit for the company. What can we do to get better managers?

John

Dear John,

When I was a manager hiring managers I always asked, "If your employees were given the opportunity to fire you, how soon would you be out the door?" The looks from the candidates would fill volumes.

A program manager I know believes strong managers motivate their employees to deliver effective solutions. He says, "When hiring managers, it is paramount to hire people who will fit the corporate culture, have a strong record of demonstrating leadership, can focus on the customer, and can think their way through difficult situations."

Hiring a new manager is a daunting task. Here are some tips from Dun and Bradstreet:

Know what you're looking for—Decide what kind of person would be a good match for your company's culture and able to work with a variety of people and personalities.

Create a "character test" – Think about specific characteristics *you* will want your new manager to have, qualities that you value in yourself.

Match skills to the role—List of all the management position's responsibilities and expect the candidate to match their skills to the requirements.

Try them out – Have final candidates shadow a manager for a day and collect employee and manager impressions.

Make the interview count—Ask penetrating questions. Provide several hypothetical scenarios that could arise on the job, and have the person explain how they would address them.

Always check references—Always be sure to thoroughly investigate a candidate's references and check out their performance at previous jobs.

Chapter Three: Getting Hired

Getting hired can be tough – and especially in today's economy. Even HR management veterans admit the job market is poor at best and they really have more candidates than they can handle whenever they post a job. In short, it is a buyer's (employer's) market.

The screening of qualified candidates and hiring just that perfect person seems to be more art than science. We have good, hard-working, and effective people who don't interview well losing positions to mediocre or poor workers, who can talk a good game.

Trust me, we al know those people who have memorized the perfect response to the typical behavioral styled questions asking, "Tell me about a time you were faced with a team challenge; what did you do, what was the outcome; and what would you do differently? Huh? Huh?"

Resumes don't tell the story, plus, no two people can agree what a great one looks like. Career coaches may help, but who has the money? Hey, even the job postings make a position look simply wonderful, when in truth it is probably a piece of crap job nobody within that company would even really want.

The saying, "It's not what you know; it's who you know" rings so true so much of the time. That's why networking and connections are so valuable. My advice to job hunters is to go out and talk to anyone who will listen to them and ask if they know about any jobs. In that same vein, volunteering gains relationships as well as serving on boards and committees. I tell my students this and they look at me like, "Are you nuts, man?"

Maybe careers and jobs are overrated in the whole scheme of things, but we must eat, so we must work. If only we could find the ideal means of matching people with skills to positions with needs for those skills. I won't even get into the need for job candidates to fit the cultures of the companies they may work for. That's another story.

Here are some questions about work and how to find it. These folks are well-intentioned beings who just want to find a job, work hard, make money, and go home and sleep at night. Is that asking too much? But first, they must impress a panel or series of hiring managers and impress them with the fact that, yes, they are that perfect person.

Dear Dave,

I have been in my job for over three years and I am at the point where I want a different job. By different I mean not a promotion within my department, but rather to do something totally different all together still using my business skills. Do you know of any research on people leaving their department to get more experience in another area of the company and then returning to their previous department with a better skill set? I am wondering is if it is beneficial for employees to get wide experience across the company rather than become an expert in one area or department?

K

Dear K,

The obvious question is, what career path and positions do you want? Whether you want to gain experience in other parts of the organization and return to your department as a well-rounded individual in a management or higher-level role, or if you aspire to move out of your department, gain diverse experience, and land a position elsewhere, you will need a plan.

I will say a diverse organizational experience can certainly lead you to new challenges and prepare you for increased leadership responsibilities throughout your organization. For example, one organization I know offers an administrative development program to select employees providing them a broad range of roles and responsibilities throughout the organization. They realize the best managers and future leaders are those who possess a broad understanding of the many groups, facets, and systems present within the clinic.

What are the tangible benefits that you can take away from a broad organizational learning experience? For one thing, you will gain a sophisticated level of knowledge and skills on diverse aspects of management, including strategic thinking and planning in a global competitive environment.

Other practical benefits include: Improved critical thinking skills, increased confidence and motivation, knowledge of the business as a whole, a long-lasting competitive edge for obtaining new roles, greater ability to lead a team and to work within a team, and enhanced communication skills

Business degrees – especially at the graduate level (MBA) – are designed to provide students with broad and diverse knowledge in many areas including finance, accounting, management, and strategy. This multifaceted approach produces well-rounded thinkers who can draw from many areas of expertise to make better decisions and more effectively solve complex problems.

This same philosophy is shared by organizations that seek to hire and promote individuals who have knowledge of many areas of the business. In that vein, your mobility within your department may be hampered due to only possessing experience and expertise within that department.

The Academy of Management reports job rotation was related to career outcomes, such as salary and promotion and is a sound strategy for career development. Sequential job movements are important for career development as identity, insight, and resilience, can be influenced by experiences gained through experiencing various roles within an organization.

The Hay Group, a global management consulting firm, reports that changing demographics are driving talent development. As the generation of baby boomers get ready to retire en-masse over the next decade many organizations are accelerating the development of leaders from among their ranks to fill vacant roles throughout the organization. Their research shows most companies want individuals who have broad experience, are adaptive, and can fill various key positions across the organization, rather than those who are only promotable within a specific department.

In short, your career development will benefit from a broad range of activities and processes providing you with varied work experiences because it increases experience, knowledge, and adaptability. Interestingly, it was found that employees who acquire new roles and experience job movement rarely if ever return to their original department. It seems they don't want to return to the farm once they have seen Paris.

Dear Dave,

Last week I interviewed for a good job and I thought I had the skills and experience needed. You won't believe the horrible questions I was asked. I was embarrassed through most of the interview and I don't think I ever really had an opportunity to sell myself. Get this question I was asked: You are a lot older than that of the position's coworkers. Is this a problem for you? Another one was, do you have kids that are sickly and how often do you need to stay home with them? Can they ask these questions? Am I over-reacting?

Peeved

Dear Peeved,

You have a right to be irritated – those are not only illegal questions, but dumb ones to ask. I hope you realize that hearing these types of questions may tell you a great deal about the management and the culture of the organization.

Illegal job interview questions include any interview questions that are related to a candidate's: age, race, ethnicity, or color, gender or sex, country of national origin, religion, disability, or marital or family status or pregnancy

One business consultant I know tells me, "Managers need to be aware of questions thought to be "harmless" but can cause legal problems. If a small business does not have an HR department they should consult their legal counsel and get expert assistance in what you can ask and what you cannot."

Various laws regulate the questions an employer can ask you. An employer's questions—on the job application or in the interview—must be related to the job for which you are applying—what the manager needs to know to decide whether or not you can perform the functions of this job.

So, how do you answer an illegal question?

If you choose to do so, realize that you are giving information that is not job-related. You could harm your candidacy by giving the "wrong" answer.

You can refuse to answer the question. You'll be within your rights, but you're also running the risk of coming off as uncooperative or confrontational – and not be viewed as the "ideal" candidate.

Examine the intent behind the question and respond with an answer as it might apply to the job.

For instance, if your interviewer asks, "Who is going to take care of your children when you have to travel?" you might answer, "I can meet the travel and work schedule that this job requires."

In conclusion, you need to stay professional even if the interviewer is not.

Dear Dave,

At my place of work there are opportunities to advance, but every time I've gone after a job I was told I do not have the education needed. So, I went back to school and earned my Bachelor's Degree, thinking this will be the ticket to get a new and more challenging position. I recently applied for a position similar to the one I did not get before I went back to school, and now I am told I do not have the experience. I suppose this cat and mouse game can go on forever. Which is more important, education or experience, and what can I do about getting enough of each to earn a new job?

Signed: Under-educated and Under-experienced

Dear Under Under,

I've got to ask this line from the movie, Airplane: Were you under Unger and Over Dunn? Sorry.

When you ask a teacher, such as yours truly, you know the answer you will get about the value of more education. However, I will answer your question with what you thought I might write and that is, get both, more education and more experience.

Now, are there a lot of people who have more degrees than a thermometer and still cannot think? Yup! Are there a lot of "experienced" people, who still do not know what they are doing? Super Yup! I had managers I was surprised were able to find their way to work each day.

Because a company CEO may have 30 years' experience and a Master's Degree in Divine Wisdom, this will not guarantee that he or she will be effective...or honest. Witness Enron, Arthur Anderson, and GM.

One manager I know believes experience and education is crucial for being hired, but there are two other critical factors that job candidates must consider. She says, "First, do your research! Learn all you can about the organization, department, and position you are interviewing for. This will show genuine interest in the organization and your research skills."

"Secondly, come to the interview equipped to share what you will BRING to the position if selected. What do you have to offer that no one else has? Why should you be considered above other candidates? All too often, candidates approach the interview with a "what's in it for me" attitude. This is a turnoff for managers and implies that your self-interest supersedes the needs of the organization."

Recommendations:

Get more education: Go back for a Master's Degree (why not?) or certificates in specific disciplines. Get a company mentor or an internship. Show company managers you want to expand your skills base through education, both inside and outside of the company.

Get more experience: Volunteer, join nonprofits and charitable groups, and try to obtain leadership positions within these organizations. The local Chamber of Commerce may have interesting groups or programs to consider.

More: Attend any in-house training your organization may have. Attend conferences, workshops and seminars. Join related professional organizations and serve on committees. Also, look for volunteer opportunities within your organization such as quality groups, process improvement teams, and committees.

Challenge: Here is something that I tell people to do and they nod their head, drooling like Pavlov's dog, and then don't do it. Build and maintain a graphic and narrative portfolio of everything you are doing to improve yourself, your accomplishments, any projects, papers, and presentations, community and organizational involvement, personal goals, and anything that will help tell your life story regarding how you are a continuous learner and have really accomplished significant things. What a great piece to bring to interviews!

For the time being: Whether you are staying with your company or looking elsewhere, make sure to do your current job well and do build great relationships. Your employee evaluations – and I hope your manager does them – will tell a tale of success, or something like what haunts me still from my grade school report cards, when the teacher wrote, "Dave visits with his neighbors too much and easily gets distracted." I still do. Make sure to work and play well with people.

Dear Dave,

Like a lot of people, I am looking for work. I have a lot of experience and skills. The same old interview format is used whenever I do finally land an interview. I am asked, tell me about a time when you faced XYZ challenge, what you did, and what were the results. How can I look better in interviews, besides having prepared answers for these obvious questions?

T

Dear T,

Yes, it seems what you are describing for interview tactics – called behavioral interviewing – is quite common and any savvy interviewee can have world class automatic, one-size-fits-all patterned responses.

You need to set yourself apart from the herd by backing up what you are saying. I have my MBA students prepare leadership portfolios that they continually update. A portfolio is a graphic presentation of your achievements, professional experiences, and anything that will display who you are, what you have done, and what you aspire to become.

Picture an artist or architect displaying their work. This is exactly what you would be doing. If the concept of a scrapbook helps you understand what this is, then picture this as building a historical scrapbook showing proof positive of your knowledge, skills, achievements, and abilities. It also shows organizational and creativity capabilities.

You could divide your portfolio into sections that may address common interview question categories such as team-building, problem-solving, leadership, management, culture building, and ethics. Also, you should consider developing an online Web-based portfolio.

What should go into it?

Here are some other basic categories. The key to remember is that you want to give reasons for the employer to hire you — you want to showcase your education and work experience by providing vivid, persuasive evidence of your work, skills, and accomplishments.

Career Summary and Goals: A description of what you stand for (such as work ethic, organizational interests, management philosophy, etc.) and where you see yourself in two to five years. Show employers you have a plan for the future and that they are your future. Include a professional philosophy/mission statement — guiding principles that drive you and give you purpose.

Resume: Stay professional, but make your resume interesting. List a summary of your education, achievements, and work experience, using a chronological or functional format. A resume should not be a War and Peace edition – keep it explanatory, but direct. I have seen many resumes so endlessly boring, I was looking for some matches.

Skills, Knowledge, Abilities and Marketable Qualities: To shine, you should offer a detailed profile of your skills and experience. This section should include the name of the skill area, the performance, knowledge, or personal traits that contribute to your success in that skill area; your background and specific experiences that demonstrate your application of the skill.

List of Accomplishments: Your accomplishments are one of the most important elements of any good job-search and employers would rather hear about what you have done than what you promise to do. Anyone can say, "Well, if you hire me, I will save the whales, feed the world, and end poverty and oppression." Yea, when Elvis gets here.

Research, Publications, Reports: This is a great way to showcase multiple skills, including your written communications abilities. Include any published papers, projects, and articles. Also, include a list of conferences, seminars, and workshops you've participated in and/or attended or a collection of any certificates of awards, honors, and scholarships.

Volunteering/Community Service: A description of any community service activities, volunteer or pro bono work you have completed, especially as it relates to your career. Showing you reach out to the community and seek to serve sends a loud message.

References List: A list of three to five people (including titles, addresses, and phone/email) who are willing to speak about your strengths, abilities, and experience. At least one reference should be a former manager. You may want to include a collection of any kudos you have received—- from customers, clients, colleagues, past employers, professors, etc. Some experts even suggest including copies of favorable employer evaluations and reviews.

Don't be bashful – tell employers who you are. People love "show and tell," so show and tell!

Dear Dave:

I am not alone when I say that landing a job right now is tough. I think I won't be able to land the perfect job. What

can I do to improve my chances of at least getting an interview for something that may be a reasonably good job?

Challenged

Dear Challenged:

This won't help, but I feel your pain. We all know that obtaining a job right now is difficult and landing that "perfect job" may be tougher than a $2 steak. First, I want you to ask 3 foundational questions:

What are my career goals?

By stopping and asking yourself that simple question, you will quickly be able to identify whether or not you are working or looking in the right area or just wasting your time. I know it is tough to examine what you want in a career when you need a job quick to pay the rent, but ultimately, you need to know where you really want to go.

How can I make myself more qualified for a position or the perfect position?

You are asking a college professor this question, so I will provide my favorite one-word answer. Are you ready? EDUCATION! It's all we have to grow and solve our problems. I don't care if you take a community ed course or enroll in a degree program, just learn and grow your knowledge and capacity to perform. This investment (though it takes time and some cash) is the smartest thing you can do. Developing your writing, speaking, planning and organizational skills can make you a stronger candidate and help you find a job. Also, you may need to start in an entry position and prove your worth to an employer. Good people will rise in a company.

How can I make connections and find a position or the perfect position?

You need to spread the word—and your resume (get your resume in shape)—in a way that doesn't tip off your current employer, if you are currently working. And you need to make sure you don't lose focus on your current job while you're searching. Attend any job fair. Volunteer to make contacts. Attend any and all community events and schmooze with people you meet. Many if not most jobs come from knowing people and not just things. Get out. Network. Rub shoulders. And ask anybody you know if they know anything about jobs anywhere. Remember, again, you may need to start in a humble job and work your way up. Finding a job may be a full-time job.

Dear Dave,

I am very under-employed in my current position and I am frustrated. I lost a great job a year ago and I mistakenly thought I would be able to get a new job quickly. I finally took a job that I really did not want, but I had to pay the bills. Unemployment was bad enough, but I think the way I feel now is worse. What can I do?

L

Dear L,

Gallup polling reports that the current unemployment rate is roughly 9.1%. Gallup also reported a surge to 9.6 in the number of part-time workers who would prefer full-time work. Combined, those two groups make an unemployment rate of 18.7.

Now, this is the tough part to calculate: Just what is the percentage of currently employed workers, such as you, who believe they are underemployed, which is defined as when an employee is overqualified and has education, experience, or skills beyond the requirements of the job they currently have?

Taking Any Job

Because of this unpredictable labor market, many laid-off professionals have been forced to take low-skilled jobs for a fraction of the pay, challenge, and prestige of their former positions.

Human resources workers tell me they often have very overqualified applicants seeking the few jobs that are available, but it is difficult to give a "routine" job to these applicants, because they know these people will become unmotivated and frustrated ... and leave or "shut-down."

Here's the part I hate: Think of all of the highly-unqualified and grossly-incompetent people we must deal with, who hold positions of authority, responsibility, and importance, that have no right or reason whatsoever being in the position they hold. Yeesh!

The Psychological Factor

Let me say – that through an act of God – the economy and job market will improve ... some time. However, in the meantime, we need to do the best we can with what we can get and stay positive.

As demeaning as it is to people to have to bear employment they would not *ordinarily* seek if conditions were good, being unemployed is a lot tougher. Being that our self-esteem is based on our feelings of self-worth, it is no wonder that being underemployed takes its mental toll.

Interestingly, there are a certain percentage of professionals who have opted to be underemployed. I have seen a significant number of people rethinking their entire life strategy and gearing down their level of employment.

What You Can Do

Realize that a great many people you know or work with have the same frustration you have, but, yet, they come to work, do their job, complete their tasks, and go home and sleep at night. There is a lot to be said for just plain having responsibilities and doing them.

Leadership writer and ex General Electric CEO, Jack Welch said, "Whatever you are, be a good one." I don't think he means if you are an axe murderer, you should "sharpen" (pun intended) your skills, but if you dig ditches in Poughkeepsie, New York, dig them suckers well!

Keep up your credentials by continuing your education. There are many educational opportunities that provide high value. And, maintain your people skills and your presence in the community by volunteering, or teaching in your area of expertise.

These things will help you feel more confident and positive, while seeking other employment opportunities. Also, keep your network healthy by using your contacts. If you are looking for the "job fairy" to sprinkle career dust on you, you're making a mistake.

Dear Dave,

My problem is huge. I was fired from a job I hated, but it wasn't because I hated the job that I got fired. I got mixed up in some employee theft problems and I should have stayed away from the people who were stealing. Instead, I kept my mouth shut and was fired because I knew and didn't come forward and report the theft. The job market is tough and my firing makes it tougher for me to find work. What can I do? What can I tell employers?

Signed, Lost

Dear Lost,

You are definitely in a pickle. I'm not sure where that pickle line came from, but I don't think I want to be in one – I digress, as usual.

Being laid off and having to find a job is tough. Being fired—for cause—and then trying to find a job is incredibly tough. However, if you have skills, experience, and are motivated, let these features help you – once again – sell yourself.

In the meantime, apply for unemployment benefits. Why? Because if there is any question about why you were fired or if your employer decides not to fight the application for benefits, you may still be able to collect.

Finding Work

It will not be easy. However, it is not insurmountable.

First and foremost, don't lie about being fired. Be honest. It's important to provide a simple explanation – "I was terminated" – and then move on. This is especially important when filling out an employment application because lying on it can be grounds for dismissal at any time.

One employment professional I know suggests you can turn the negative into a positive. She says, "If asked, you should briefly explain why you were terminated, acknowledge that you now know you made some bad decisions, then explain what you have learned and how you've changed. Not every employer will give you a chance, but some will appreciate the honesty and openness."

Practice interviewing and make sure your story is convincing and sincere. You may need to begin with temporary work. Getting a temporary job is a good way to get a foot in the door at a local employer.

Consider small, local employers. An independently-owned and operated business person often has a more open mind and willingness to forgive than large corporations.

Also, commit to these two major don'ts:

1. Don't lie.
2. Don't insult or blame your former boss or your former employer.

Regardless of what happened in the past, focus on the skills and experience you have, rather than the firing.

Dear Dave,

Maybe other people have the problem I have. I am unable to be promoted or even transfer within my company because I am just too good in my job. Nobody has come out and said that, but I know it is a fact. Management looks to me as being the expert in the work I do. I would love to advance at our company, but I think I have over-worked my way into a corner.

K

Dear K,

Your problem is more common than you think. I will warn you upfront that the last thing you want to do is start decreasing the quality and amount of work you do in an effort to get promoted – that would be nonsense and would absolutely backfire.

Admittedly, when I was a manager, I always feared the fact my "stars" would expect to move on. How dare these performers show desire to advance … just when things were clicking like a fine Swiss watch. In hindsight, that was very selfish of me.

With this understanding, I know many other managers must have the same thoughts – thus, your dilemma. Great people are hard to find and you don't want to lose them. However, true leaders would never stand in the way of someone wishing to better themselves and would support them without exception.

The Management Perspective

I would bet your boss knows your desire to grow within the company. There may be reasons why he or she is not acting on your desire at the current moment. Maybe the company needs you to work on what you are doing – your effectiveness may be more important for the business then your desire.

There is also the possibility that management may feel you are not ready for the move into management or a higher position. Maybe they are actually telling you that you may need to grow more and gain more experience in your current position before they are comfortable moving you up.

For You

Stay productive and positive. If you are looking for a position with more responsible duties, keep doing great with what you are doing, and take on additional tasks and responsibility that may not necessarily be in your job description, and continue to do your best with a positive attitude.

You didn't tell me if you liked your company or your job. If not, there are always other jobs out there. Look into going back to school to increase your skills and exposure to the job market. Update your resume and submit it to jobs that have the management responsibilities that you are looking for.

If you really like the company you are working for, at your next evaluation, find out what is required to become a manager at your company. Patience, continuing to work very hard, and continuing education on a regular basis will eventually put you in a win-win situation.

In the meantime, why don't you ask for a salary increase? If your employer is keen to retaining their best people, and promotion isn't on the cards, it would be to your advantage to ask for better remuneration.

Also, don't badger your bosses for a promotion, or they may think that a job title is more important than your desire to work for the company—no one likes hearing constant complaining.

For right now I would remain patient and do what you are doing the best most professional way you can. Good thing do happen to people who wait.

Dear Dave,

Where I work there are opportunities to advance, but every time I interview I get the"behavioral interview questions", which always make me feel like I am not able to really explain how good I wood be in the position. I know that it is important to know about things like my experiences, but I get so involved in providing the perfect answer, that the real me does not come out. What can I do?

Signed: K

Dear K,

I know exactly what you mean, because I have been in the same self-representation struggles when interviewing. The fact is, there are no perfect ways to "screen" job candidates. Your company means well, because they want to hear about what you did and learned in various situations.

Some people come into the job interview with a great deal of education and experience, which gives them a leg up when conjuring up answers to behavioral questions. They have more to reflect back on so to speak, including work experiences, study situations and achievements, and problem-solving encounters.

Now, are there a lot of people who have more degrees than a thermometer and still cannot think? Yup! Are there a lot of "experienced" people, who still do not know what they are doing? Super Yup! I had managers I was surprised were able to find their way to work each day, but they talked a good game.

Being the Best You

I believe experience and education is crucial for being hired, but there are two other critical factors that you must consider. First, do your research! Learn all you can about the organization, department, and position you are interviewing for. This will show genuine interest in the organization and your research skills.

Secondly, come to the interview equipped to share what you will BRING to the position if selected. What do you have to offer that no one else has? Why should you be considered above other candidates? All too often, candidates approach the interview with a "what's in it for me" attitude — this is a turnoff for many managers I know.

As you may already be doing, think about and rehearse your responses to behavioral interview questions. You should have prepared responses for the very common question realms such as teams, situation handling, communicating, and project management. But, be honest and listen carefully when the question is posed and when the interviewers are talking.

Other Recommendations:

Discuss your education and fit it into your responses.: If you went back for a degree, find a way to mention this. Also, tell the hiring managers you want to expand your skills base through education, both inside and outside of the company on a continuing basis.

Discuss your experience and don't be shy: If you have done exemplary things and had great evaluations, make sure to talk about these. If you had taken on a leadership role in some project, make sure this is mentioned. If your evaluations show you are strong in team work, mention this when there is an opening.

Challenge: Here is something that I tell people to do and they nod their head, drooling like Pavlov's dog, and then don't do it: build and maintain a graphic and narrative portfolio of everything you are doing to improve yourself,

Include your accomplishments, any projects, papers, and presentations, community and organizational involvement, personal goals, and anything that will help tell your life story regarding how you are a continuous learner and have really accomplished significant things. What a great piece to bring to interviews!

Chapter Four: Favoritism

I suppose it is only human nature that someone plays favorites. The likelihood of liking one person over another or others is a fact of life. However, favoritism in the workplace is an act punishable by being flogged by a large organizational human resource guide.

For whatever reason(s) we would choose to treat different people differently, there really is no excuse for not having a balanced system of fairness in the workplace when it comes to hiring, promotions, participation, and general every-day care and treatment.

We stereotype. We have biases. And, we are quick to judge. It's only human nature. But, consider all of the talented, creative people there are in the world who are not given a level playing field of opportunities or consideration simply because they are not "liked" by someone in power. Can I say, Geesh!

Psychologists call what we do when we cast our beliefs and dispersions about one person on to another, transference. Someone may remind us of someone we like – or do not – and people may remind us of ourselves, and accordingly, will then receive a very biased version of treatment from us. We may favor that person or we may treat them like crap – and we do not even know why, nor do we *want to* think about it.

Favoritism is rampant in the workplace. I, myself have bore the brunt of favoritism and have also been a cheerful recipient of it. Suffice it to say that even though we claim to be rationale and objective thinkers, we are not; rather, we are emotional, biased, and prejudicial animals that like what we like … damn it!

I'm hoping, just hoping, that by reading about some of these "favoritism" struggles from folks in their jobs we may gain a better understanding of ourselves and others when it comes to uneven treatment of people, because of liking. Let's visit a few examples from the past.

Dear Dave,

My boss has different rules for different people when hiring people, though rules are clearly spelled out in our personnel manual. Hiring is supposed to be frozen, yet he hires people and the jobs are not even posted anywhere, almost always placing some employees' friends in the jobs. What is going on here?

R

Dear R,

What is going on here is just what you stated: different rules and treatment for different people, as well as taking the liberty to hire despite the freeze. From my experience in the organizational and business environment, this is frowned on, but it does happen.

There is a clear case of favoritism occurring when he is hiring without posting the positions and selecting employees based on the friendship they have with some employees. What baffles me is how he is able to hire during a freeze, which leads me to believe he is very well connected in your company and receives special treatment and consideration.

Unfortunately, some managers will conduct these "backdoor" hiring methods, making the playing field for advancement quite uneven for current employees. For whatever reasons, he is convinced this is the way hiring should be done … and he is getting away with it.

Equal Opportunity

Favoritism has always been a complaint and issue in hiring. In a recent survey from the federal government's Office of Personnel Management, it was found that only 36.1% of federal workers thought promotions in their work units were based on merit. In short, they believed that connections, partisanship, and other factors played a role.

Aristotle has a lot to say about fairness: "Equals should be treated equally and unequals unequally." This means there needs to be objective criteria used when hiring and everyone that should be considered is considered and has an equal opportunity to relate their skills and experience when seeking a position. My experience with most managers is they tend to follow company hiring guidelines fairly well.

When someone is granted a position because of connections, rather than because he or she has the best credentials and experience, their work may be inferior. It is quite risky to hire people that may not only be ineffective, but will hurt the company and the reputation of the manager.

I will state, though, that some – even most – of the best hires I have made in my management career were referred candidates from trusted employees. Of course, the candidates had the skills and background necessary to be successful in the position, but they also had the backing of reputable employees that were going out on a limb to endorse them. Referrals are powerful.

Bypassing the normal recruitment process is unfair to both internal staff seeking promotional opportunities and outside candidates looking to work for the company. However, remember, favoritism in the workplace is not illegal, just unfair, uncertain, and unhealthy.

For You

You might question if it is worth a fight in your present job. You need to decide if it is better to end your association with a company that accepts favoritism.

This sort of treatment can occur in pretty much any office environment, large or small. How you react to it really depends on how blatant it is and whether or not it's illegal. Plus, any career options you have moving forward might also dictate how you respond. Your company's willingness to tolerate such behavior says a great deal, especially if it appears that they promote it, or at least tolerate it.

If the favoritism you are witnessing is holding you back, or hurting you, and you feel it is based on illegal reasons—race, sex, age, etc.—you might consider legal action, but you'd obviously need proof of wrong doing to have a case.

Instead, you can get further if you focus on your work, stay positive, and take responsibility for creating a more positive work environment for yourself and others around you. Also, I believe your boss' practices will come to an end when the right people catch wind of it.

I appreciate that the work environment you describe is demoralizing. However, nobody can keep you at the bottom of the heap when you are doing top notch work and come to work every day with a positive attitude – that is what will get you noticed and promoted.

Dear Dave,

Favoritism runs rampant at my workplace. I know I will never be a teacher's pet and I don't want to be, but, I don't want to be treated differently and lesser than others. People get promoted here and it is not because of their skills. Without becoming a "brown-noser" what can I do?

S

Dear S,

First, let's take a look at the definition of "favoritism." Basically, favoritism is just what it sounds like; it's favoring a person, not because he or she is doing the best job but, rather, because of manager personal likes and dislikes, or friendship.

In business, favoritism can be demonstrated in hiring, awarding contracts, promotions, special rewards, etc. I recall Tommy Smothers of the Smothers Brothers — I'm sure less than half of my readers will remember this - telling his brother, Dick, "Mom always liked you best." Thus, favoritism, or the belief it is happening, is everywhere, even in the family.

As the old saying goes, "It's not what you know, but who you know," or, as one of my colleagues puts it, "The "good ol' boys club" takes care of one another."

Favorites Get Favors

Here's one I really hate: People will boast, "I'm on the fast track at my company!" What the heck does that mean ... everyone else is on the dog track? I heard my brother-in-law tell me once that he was a "fast tracker" – he is a smart man – and his "fast track" led him to a layoff.

I do believe some people are more promotable, especially if they show the attitude and the aptitude to be promotable. I especially like companies that "promote from within" and give internal job candidates the edge over candidates from the outside. But, this assumes these inside people are qualified and not just "favored".

The "Unfavorites"

How many times have you or someone you know at work say, "Well, we all knew he or she would get the job and we know why (wink wink)." As much as we try to blow it off, favoritism hurts, and it cuts deeper than we realize. I wonder how many "favorites" really feel good about themselves if they get this or that, because they are favored, and do not really excel over other people – maybe they feel nothing.

Sadly, the "Unfavorites" watch things happen, such as: witnessing time and again you have to be on a "fast track" program in order to be promoted; favorites are chosen for a development program"behind closed doors"; some employees have been identified as non-promotable, regardless of job performance; and some are given more interesting assignments, even though others are more qualified.

Coping Suggestions

First, you must understand that bosses don't like it when people question or ridicule their decisions – even if favoritism is so blatantly obvious in whatever thinking they did do to make a human resources decision.

Also, while it may be hard to keep our attitudes in check in the interest of job security, you must be aware of how and if you convey your disgruntled feelings. Take responsibility for your actions and don't place blame on others. Also, take more initiative and push yourself to work a little harder than usual.

And – by all means – stay positive! Nobody likes perpetual "Debbie Downers" even if they have a valid point. I'm not saying you need to be phony and network by "kissing ..."; I am saying that bright, industrious, positive people will be recognized by managers who can see beyond their "crony nose."

Dear Dave:

The owner of our company just brought his oldest son onboard and gave him an executive position. I have been with the company for 18 years and have watched this guy grow up – at least physically grow up. He does have a college degree, but he has no people skills. He was always spoiled rotten and never put in a day's work. How can I deal with this? I know there are going to be many mistakes made and I do not want to see the company hurt.

Signed: Frustrated

Dear Frustrated,

In defense of Junior, maybe he has matured and learned something. Give him a shot and see what he is made of. The risk you run is he will mess up and cause damage to the company. If the father is a savvy business person – I assume he is, because you have stuck with him for 18 years – he will keep an eye on junior and monitor his behavior.

If you have an open and honest relationship with the father, ask for a private meeting and very diplomatically voice your concerns about the direction of the company. Be careful, you will be voicing a concern based on speculation and you have no proof things may need watching.

Also, remember, parents are *usually* proud of their kids and want to see them do well. The parents believe it is a lasting legacy for their children to carry the torch onward.

Business consultant, Will Schroter, offers some advice:

1. Give them a chance – Before you jump to conclusions about their capabilities, give them at least a few months to not only get a feel for what they can accomplish, but how the rest of the organization deals with their new role.

2. See things from their perspective – They may be as sensitive to the nepotism issue as you are. Give them a chance to offer their perspective before assuming they are ungrateful for their leg up.

3. Make them successful – Anything you can do to make it obvious to your boss that you are doing everything in your power to help make them successful will score major points for you in the process (and create an ally with this new person).

4. Show them the ropes – Like any new employee, this new person will likely need some guidance about the organization and this is a good opportunity to show

that you're a team player and make a powerful friend in the organization.

5. Remember who hired them—Remember, the parents may have pressured them to come onboard and grow and thrive. The parents do not want to look bad, so don't make them.

See what happens. You may be surprised. In any case, know that Dad will be watching closely. There is no way he wants to see his labor fail. He will "not let go of the bicycle" until he is assured his son can stay up and in a straight line. Good luck.

Chapter Five: Change

Change. It's inevitable. In order to stay the same, you need to change. Though many people fight like mad to avoid change, they can't. If you look back fifty years, think about how people, fashion, cars, food, lifestyles, and countless other things have changed. Like death, taxes, and time, you can't escape change.

Managers and their employees are expected to change, deal with change, look for new changes, and change past changes. Managed well, change can be healthy for you and your company, leading to improved profit margins, happier and more productive employees, and a stable and growing company. Managed poorly, it can lead to poor morale, loss in production, and ultimately the possibility of bankruptcy.

People resist change for more reasons than I get detail, but the major compelling reason people resist is not the change itself; it's the fact they may/will need to change. No wonder so many people are afraid of change!

There are many reasons why over 70% of change initiatives fail to perform up to expectations. Many experts state change needs both leadership to guide the flock through the perils of change, and constant communication – explaining the why and the how of the change.

New ideas, procedures and technology involve risk and it is not be possible to always succeed. Great intentions and good decisions can have bad outcomes, and how an organization reacts to a failed attempt to implement a change is critical.

If people are punished, belittled, or put down for trying something new that doesn't work, the will be seldom willing to do it again. If, on the other hand, efforts are made to learn from the failure and to make it work a more open process of change will occur.

I, myself, resist change all the time, but when I look back I realize—most of the time – the change was for the better. However, don't tell my wife that, because every stitch of clothing I own – that she loathes seeing on me – will be in a Goodwill bag faster than blink your eye.

Let's explore some change situations.

Dear Dave,

At my company, there have been a lot of changes and many of them are not pleasant, but we all cope the best we can. It just seems everything is thrown on us without any explanation of why the change is happening and what we need to do to. I hope my manager reads this, because this is creating a lot of tension for all of us and we talk about it every day.

K

Dear K,

Philosopher, Frederich Nietzsche said, "Tell the people the *why* and they will determine the *how*." In short, people may not mind the change, and even will get busy to support the change, if they understand why the change is needed.

You and your fellow employees have a "whys and how" problem—you neither understand the rationale behind the change (assuming there is one), nor are you prepared to implement whatever the change is.

People don't come to work as mindless robots (some will debate me on this) and they really want to contribute, master what they do, and fit into the collective effort to get things done. To do these things, employees need the whys and the how.

So, What Should We Do?

We know that motivation is dependent on employees being in the know." According to a study referenced in a recent *Wall Street Journal* article, employees of companies that explained decisions more fully were more than twice as likely to support decisions as workers who received less information.

How hard is it to explain to someone why something is proposed, or what the logic is behind a decision? Is it that hard to finish a sentence such as, "Do this!" with something as simple as "… because it will provide us/you this …?"

Further, what if managers would make a statement that provides even further evidence for the change rationale and also show respect for the employee who will be dealing with the change? It could be as simple as saying, "We found that change XYZ would be beneficial to our/your productivity and performance, because of yada yada and we need your support in making the change happen by yada yada."

Dare we go a step further? I see even greater things happening and employees being even more motivated when management provides a consultative and joint problem solving approach by getting feedback and input from employees (those folks close to the task to begin with) when discussing a change and why it is being proposed.

Just last night, some of my MBA students and I discussed the need for managers to ask employees for ideas about implementing a change, and discuss and use their ideas. What a concept!

How do you cope?

As always, be thankful you have a job – I can't say that enough. Be patient, listen carefully and respectfully when management is dealing out or recommending a change, and politely ask how you and your fellow employees can be creative and innovative to help the change become successful.

Explain you want to help the company succeed and you realize the many limitations, stresses, and constraints the company is dealing with in this turbulent business environment. Because of all this, you want to make sure you do the right things the right ways and that you even have some ideas.

This positive attitude bodes well with managers and you will feel more contributive and less adversarial to company change ambitions, thus, standing a better chance of keeping your job. End of story.

Dear Dave,

I hear so much about change and companies must know when and how to change. I am sure every company has room for growth and improvement, but what do you look for that can tell you if change is needed? My company seems to be doing OK and most people seem to be somewhat satisfied to work here. Maybe I am missing the forest for the trees.

Signed: Change Challenged

Dear Challenged,

Companies must constantly analyze how they are doing things and if there is a need to change what they are doing by learning and implementing new practices. Leadership expert, Warren Bennis said, "In order to stay the same, you have to change."

Employees and managers must constantly be on the prowl for practices that are being used, which should be modified or even discontinued. Also, the company must be looking at other companies that are having great success to discover what they are doing and how they gauge and measure success. This benchmarking can help a company discover things they could or should be doing.

There are a wide variety of reasons for reorganizing any sized organization, particularly in today's rapidly changing marketplace. However, there are several reasons for reorganization that seem to keep coming up in both for-profit and nonprofit businesses. These reasons include, but are not limited to:

- o An employee keeps complaining (and you agree) that he or she is overloaded with work.
- o Employees complain that their activities overlap and confusion is resulting.
- o Employees do not have enough work to do during a work day.
- o Employees complain that they're reporting to more than one boss, or supervisor.
- o Management notices a large amount of employee turnover.
- o A department, or major function in the organization, has recurring problems.
- o Customer complaints are mounting.
- o Supplier problems are present.
- o Sales are down and costs are up.

Attempts at change or reorganizing may be just fine tuning, or tweaking, if not done with the long term in mind. In fact, the recurring problems may be a symptom of the organization's not having clearly thought out what its overall purpose and goals are. Without visiting the overall purpose and goals, redesign is usually a highly reactive and very short-term fix. Carefully consider conducting a strategic planning process to guide your actions and moves.

Successful change must involve top management, including the president and chief executive. Change is usually best carried out as a team-wide effort. Communications about the change should be frequent and with all organization members. To sustain change, the structures of the organization itself should be modified, including strategic plans, policies and procedures.

The best approach to address resistance that often appears in change initiatives is through increased and sustained communication and education. For example, the leader should meet with all managers and staff to explain reasons for the change, how it generally will be carried out, and where others can go for additional information.

A plan should be developed and communicated. Communicate why the change is taking place. Meetings should be held so organizational members can express their ideas and suggestions. They should be able to express their concerns and frustrations as well, because getting these out in the open is required for change to become embedded.

Other Suggestions

o Consider using a consultant who is highly experienced in organization-wide change.
o Widely communicate the potential need for change. Communicate what you're doing about it.
o Communicate what is going to happen, what was done, and how it worked out.
o Get as much feedback as practical from employees, customers, and suppliers, including what they think are the problems and what should be done to resolve them. If possible, work with a team of employees to manage the change.
o Don't get wrapped up in doing change for the sake of change. Know why you're making the change. What goal(s) do you hope to accomplish?
o Plan the change. How do you plan to reach the goals, what will you need to reach the goals, how long might it take and how will you know when you've reached your goals or not.
o Delegate decisions to employees as much as possible. As much as possible, let them decide how to do a project.

In summary, change is necessary and should be a continuous process. Organizations need to learn and use change methods to ensure they are competitive and productive.

Dear Dave:

I have read your articles about what management experts say about how to handle employees with change, but I don't see you mention the effects of change on managers. We get stressed too. Sometimes the managers get fired during change. How do managers cope with change?

Bill

Dear Bill:

Yup, you are correct. I apologize for not paying more attention to the managers and their struggles to not only promote change, but stay positive when change is making their life very difficult. My wife and I just saw the George Clooney movie, "Up in the Air" and I have renewed my appreciation for the emotional conflicts anyone goes through when change such as layoffs occur.

Like employees, managers are subject to the same reactions, emotions, and struggles, and change, such as restructuring, or downsizing can put considerable strain on managers. Not only does the manager have to deal with the change and find ways to make change happen, but they must sell the change to reluctant employees and be cheerleaders of the change, even though they may have doubts themselves.

One manager I know states that when changes take place, managers must get employees on board with the decision. However, if managers don't agree with the change, there is a natural internal conflict experienced. Then, managers can either swallow hard and go along, or try to persuade executives to rethink their strategy.

The stress can be intense. In the case of downsizing, stress levels surge, because the manager is given the chore of letting people go. To make things worse, ineffective managers may not handle change well, which increases stress, which reduces change effectiveness even more.

Stress Increases — We cannot assume that managers are blessed with special powers that make them immune to the effects of change. Change stress, if mishandled, can result in loss of managerial effectiveness. Thus, managers need to be alert to the signs of stress upon their attitudes, performance, emotions, and their thinking, and not be afraid to seek help to cope with the stresses.

Denial Occurs — Often, managers may simply avoid involvement in change when that involvement is unpleasant. The effects of this detachment can be lethal to the willingness and ability of the employees to promote change. If managers under-estimate or even deny the impact of the change, and demonstrate an inability to respond to employees' emotional reactions to change, this creates a vicious cycle of mistrust, resistance, and fear. Sorry for this line: "Denial is not a river in Egypt."

Self-Assessment — Management writer, Ken Blanchard states it is important for managers to anticipate and respond to employee concerns and feelings. However, managers must also self-assess their own emotional responses to change. When planning for and anticipating change, managers must include a detailed reaction analysis. Managers must try to identify the kinds of reactions and questions that employees will have, but they must also look at the concerns and questions they themselves may have about the change, and their ability to promote the change and stay positive.

Remember that the success of any change rests with the ability of the managers as leaders to address both the emotional and practical issues of change. Seeking help from other managers is not a sign of weakness; rather, it is a strength and just plain smart.

Dear Dave,

I cannot get people to support the change needs we have. My employees know when things are wrong and need fixing. However, when we talk about solutions, this is when everyone gets real nervous and ducks the issues. I guess the change itself is the toughest part. Trust me, I have read and heard so much about how to bring about change, but I still have problems. I know there are not magical solutions, but I must be missing something. What can I do?

B

Dear B,

There is a great deal you can do. We have witnessed organizations that have changed not only in terms of a new destination, but have increased their capacity to deal with change. These companies include Google, Microsoft, Apple, Starbucks, and FedEx.

Leadership author, John Kotter, says the first step in change is to create a "sense of urgency," where everyone realizes that the change is not only important, but must be addressed quickly.

I personally believe in the "shock factor," where staff are jolted to reality and recognize if something is not done (change), the company – and they—will suffer. I don't mean you should create debilitating paranoia, but everyone must believe change cannot be avoided.

Successful change management is possible when management prepares the employees for change needs. This is termed *change readiness*. You have to encourage employees to accept change, but they will embrace it more if they feel "ready." Change readiness includes the following dimensions:

Communications and information exchange: Determine how well you are communicating purpose, details, and goals of changes. Surface and minimize false perceptions, inaccurate gossip, and outright resistance.

Employee Involvement: Participation is not a choice. If employees are involved, they will create a future that already has them in it. People support what they create. No, even more — people *only* support what they create.

Preparation for Change: Raising confidence in the ability to use new processes or technology can be a very valuable tool in promoting acceptance of change. For training to be successful, however, there must be an understanding of how training supports the change goals.

Attitudes towards Change: Previously acquired negative attitudes towards change have significant impact on the likelihood of change acceptance. Erase these inhibiting attitudes by providing the "why" of the change and how the change makes sense.

Manage Impressions: Are your change initiatives succeeding in the eyes of employees? Do they know what signs will tell them if they are succeeding at making the desired change? Employee support and actions will continue if they can identify the signs of success. Take advantage of change momentum and let employees know the wheels are turning. Oh…also celebrate successes!

Motivation: First, be honest and identify the possible risks that may be encountered, so, if and when they occur, employees don't have the pejeepers scared out of them. Also, divide the change initiative into bite-size, doable, and actionable pieces. Remember, the best way to eat an elephant is one bite at a time.

In addition, there must be a zero tolerance for blame! In the search to understand possible failure, a lot of blame can get assigned. One healthcare executive I know recently stated, "We're under so much stress that often we try to find somebody we can shoot. People must assume responsibility for their work."

I strongly believe that change failures are the result of some very deep misunderstandings of what's going on inside organizations. If we can clear up these misunderstandings, change can happen. Show employees the change makes sense, include them early and often, and explain the personal value of the change.

Chapter Six: Workplace

If you did a Google search of business processes, management challenges, and employee satisfaction you would receive literally thousands of pages of information on how to manage the workforce. You can assume there truly is a demand to find a magic wand that will ease our personnel troubles and make employees happy as clams.

However, managers are hard-pressed to discover and fulfill employee needs when it comes to those crucial areas of compensation, motivation and productivity, job satisfaction, career development, and training and education. Even more crucial within the management domain is recruiting and hiring stellar employees who are above average and do superior work … without complaining, no less.

Without competent, satisfied, and motivated people in key roles a business will not grow, nor produce to its potential. Yet, more often than not, we hire and promote people with no experience or background in management at all, and certainly not HR experience.

In a study done by the Hay Group, just 40% of employees commended their company on retaining high quality workers. 41% agreed that performance evaluations were fair. 58% rated their job training as favorable. Most said they have few opportunities for advancement-and they didn't know in any case, what was required to move up. Most telling, only half the workers below the manager level believed their companies took a genuine interest in their well-being (Fast Company, August 2005). Let me say this, Yikes!

Managers have it tough and are under pressure. They are expected to create and maintain an excellent workforce yet do not see, nor are they given clear ways to meet that objective. I try to solve management dilemmas – I really do! Here are a couple situations to peruse. You be the judge if Dave is on the mark or writing more rants to fill the pages.

Dear Dave:

At my company, more and more people are being offered the opportunity to do their job from home. Personally, I don't think I would be as productive working from home. What are your views on this trend and are home workers able to be as productive as they are in the office?

T

Dear T,

Contrary to popular belief, it's not a lack of discipline, nor even the notion that people who work from home (termed telecommuting or teleworking) will be less productive that makes this work-life balance a challenge. It's really our tendency toward "workaholism" – we will be consumed and become obsessed by the fact our work is sitting right in front of us.

One work-from-home employee I know tells me a great story about his entrapment. He says he gets up early and on my way to the coffee maker, he sees his computer sitting on the table and thinks he'll just check his email quick. He finds it's three hours later and he's still sitting at the computer in his bathrobe working, and realizes he's had no shower and coffee.

What Can Happen

This is no secret: when you work from home, it's inevitable that some of your personal life will seep into your office. Possibly, something needs fixing, your cat's on the keyboard, your child's crying, or your neighbor calls you to play golf (that offer is a tough one).

Some people report they feel like they don't have the privacy they need at home. Others say they feel isolated and alone. Still others report they are not taken as seriously when their communications are from home. Finally, some report that their inability to separate their work—life from their home life strains their family relationships.

However, the trend for many companies is to provide employees the opportunity to work at home. Economically, it makes perfect sense. But, not all people are cut out to work from home for many different reasons including: a lack of self-motivation and discipline, a need to be with people to think and work, or, simply, they want to keep their work at work.

Some telecommuters simply miss the usual social interaction, so they tend to over-communicate, making more phone calls to check up and following up all comments with e-mails. They have "techno cabin fever."

The Advantages

First, employers like it, because costs are reduced. In a study of companies that have telecommuting employees involving California computer technology companies, an average of about 23% of the employees work from home at least once a week. Of those people, more than half do it full time. The company benefits from happier employees and customers also benefit by getting service beyond traditional work schedules.

Companies find telecommuting employees have improved morale—people love autonomy and flexibility—and this style of work is perfect for the freedom it provides.

Also, studies have shown employers benefit from less sick and personal leave taken; lower turnover, which cuts hiring and training costs; reduced office and parking space needs; and increased employee productivity. Different companies have measured increases in productivity between 10 and 35% among their employees who work remotely.

Finally, telecommuting can create jobs for nontraditional workers, such as, the disabled, new parents, or residents of remote areas.

A Culture Change

One of the largest obstacles to expanding telecommuting is that it represents a culture shift in businesses and for the many managers that only trust what they see ... employees sitting at their computer working away.

One business consultant I know said managers should focus on "deliverables" and quantifiable measures that show whether an employee is doing a good job. He believes that telecommuting programs will only work if managers value results, not time spent on work.

Accordingly, it is advised that managers should hold regular staff meetings and bring the telecommuters in to share their accomplishments, discuss ideas, and generally, to just mingle and interact live. Otherwise, the workers could be found in their front yard talking to a tree,

Some telecommuters feel they are out of the loop on what is going on in the company, so it is advised that telecommuters find a co-worker at the office who will call them with relevant news, work updates, or even grapevine talk.

Telecommuting is projected to keep growing, but companies and workers need to do research and decide if the arrangement will work for them.

Dear Dave,

I am a manager for a healthcare organization. How can I get my people to quit wasting work time and also to quit wasting their time on things that seem to add little value to what must get done? I know I can just command them to quit wasting their time and to move on to the big priorities, but I would rather treat them with more respect and convince them their work focus is extremely important and that some of the

things they do are not that important. My boss says our department productivity is down, so I need to fix this soon.

P

Dear P,

I know exactly what you are asking and I have managed people who were skilled artisans at wasting time and I have also been managed by masters of misguided priorities, poor project skills, and a plethora of personality flaws I don't even care to get into.

I will tell you upfront that maximizing productivity while bringing out the very best in your people – plus not micromanaging their souls away—is job-one for a manager. Wasting time can become epidemic and a well-ingrained part of the culture, making remediation even more difficult.

Here are some facts: A survey of 2,057 employees by online compensation company Salary.com found that about six in every 10 workers admit to wasting time at work with the average employee wasting 1.7 hours of a typical 8.5 hour working day. Personal Internet use, socializing with co-workers, and conducting personal business are the biggest time wasters.

Managing Time Wasters

Most managers are aware some employees waste their time at work. Dealing with such employees is often difficult if they do succeed in getting their work done during the working hours. If you say something, their thoughts are, "Hey, get off my case. I'm getting the work done!" However, how much more could be done, or improved, if employees spent less time wasting time?

You need to do some research. There are always reasons why people waste their time at work. It could be they are not satisfied with their job, they're bored, they got skipped-over for a promotion, the demands are actually too stressful, or their salary is so low that they will only contribute what they think they are being paid for. Then, you may have a motivation or a resentment problem and you need to find a way to get and keep these employees engaged and active.

I suggest you find the real reasons and devise a plan to get these people more interested in their job and to realize the importance of their contributions to the department and company. They can even become more challenged through job expansion and skill development. Of course, if your motivation plan doesn't work, then it is time to consider getting the free riders off the bus.

For the Priority Challenged Souls

As a manager, it is a priority to clarify priorities. Maybe you need to return to the basics and conduct some mini education sessions addressing fundamentals including: discussing the purpose of their jobs, how they are measured for effectiveness, what excellence is, what the specific priorities and deadlines are, the availability of resources, and how what they do impacts other people and other work.

Get off to a fresh start with these employees by revisiting the foundations of time management and the obstacles keeping people from concentrating their strengths on what needs to be done. Also, recognize them for doing work well and on time. Possibly, your HR dept. can provide training on time management. A planner and "to do" list can work wonders, too.

Also, make sure your goals and the goals of your employees are in total sync and are fully understood. Set a meeting with the employees, individually and/or as a group, and obtain full agreement that the goals you are setting make sense. Help them see that the timely execution of their tasks affect each and every other employee. Sometimes, people just need to see the importance of their work and how it contributes to the success of the organization.

Finally, your job is to improve individual, team, and organizational performance by setting clear and concise employee expectations, motivating workers, monitoring progress, aligning measurable individual goals with larger organizational goals, and recognizing and rewarding individual accomplishments. Do these things and no time will be wasted.

Dear Dave,

Where I work, diversity is talked about, but we don't do a very good job of respecting diverse employees. In fact, what people say in private about other nationalities and races would make your head spin. I try my best to respect all others who work here. I think it is the fault of management that we have this problem.

R

Dear R,

Yes, it is the fault of management and, yes, it is a huge problem that must be solved and solved permanently. If it isn't, not only will your workplace be an extremely uncomfortable place to be, but talented people will leave.

Inclusiveness is making room for everyone in a place of work; thus differentiating between a workplace that is just simply diverse to being a workplace that values diversity. Managers must learn to implement strategies and tools to help create an environment that is welcoming to all.

It is also management's responsibility to engage in preventing discrimination and promoting diversity. In that same vein, it is also the responsibility of each and every employee to respect the rights of every individual and to never discriminate.

What is Workforce Diversity?

Diversity in the workplace means bringing together people of different ethnic backgrounds, religions, age groups, and other diverse groups into a cohesive and productive unit. In order to survive, a company needs to be able to manage and utilize its diverse workplace effectively. Managing diversity in the workplace should be a part of the culture of the entire organization as well as a management mandate.

Diversity in the workplace is generally regarded as a positive for companies that manage it effectively. However, a workforce that has significant differences in ethnicity, race, religion, gender, and other individual differences can produce negative effects, if not well-managed.

These negative effects of diversity happen if the work culture does not support tolerance and acceptance of differences. However, most companies that intentionally hire a diverse workforce have human resources processes in place to manage diversity.

Go to Management

I urge you to go to your management with your observations and concerns. Left untreated the situation can become worse and affect the productivity and well-being of all workers. The environment will grow to be more resentful and toxic.

Tell management the organization needs to train their employees about diversity and its usefulness to the well being of the corporation. Diversity training is a critical part when managing diversity.

According to one HR manager I know , employees need to "understand and value" of the differences among them. The acceptance of differences in a positive manner is critical if the corporation is keen to enable innovation thorough creative thinking in the workplace.

Please do not fall victim to the culture you describe. Model good inclusion practices and avoid conversations that are exhibiting bias and prejudice. Even go so far as to tell coworkers your are uncomfortable with discriminatory dialogue and you would prefer they not pursue it. You may not win friends, but you will sleep better at night.

Your employer has an obligation to provide employees with a safe work environment free from discrimination, harassment and intimidation. Without the proper training and management, a diverse workplace can become a breeding ground for behavior and actions that rise to the level of unlawful and unfair employment practices.

Therefore, employers have several responsibilities concerning diversity in the workplace. Employers have a responsibility to practice – not just advertise –inclusiveness.

Dear Dave,

My company has tried to save money by getting rid of people, who not only performed well, but also made our customers quite happy to do business with us. Our customer service was once truly outstanding, but the cuts have made our service suffer to the point we have lost several customers. Why can't management understand that these cuts are only hurting business?

P

Dear P,

Business evolves around people serving people. When there are less people serving customers the quality of customer care will disintegrate faster than an ice cube on the sun.

This, in turn, will cost companies valuable customers who would love to continue doing business with them, but now sense a betrayal of neglect. There is not one of us who has not received lousy customer service in stores or on the phone because of a lack of qualified trained service staff.

What makes a company successful in the long term is its service, innovation, management, and products. All of these do not happen without good people. From a short-term perspective layoffs make the company more viable, but from a long-term perspective it can seriously damage the culture and affect the good people who you need to run the business in the future.

In short, the shareholders are the ones who will suffer in the long run. The talent will leave. Sales and revenue will continue to drop. The shareholders will be left with a worthless product produced by highly-stressed, nervous, unmotivated employees. Finally, customers are not blind; they notice the drops in quality and service.

What Layoffs Mean

Companies now routinely cut workers even when profits are rising. Some troubled industries seem to be in perpetual downsizing mode. But,, there is research suggesting that firms incur big costs when they cut workers. Some of these costs are obvious, such as the direct costs of severance and outplacement, and some are intuitive, such as the toll on morale and productivity as anxiety infects remaining workers.

There are other short-term costs to consider. For instance, it takes time to process people out. Managers have to take the time to sit down and break the news to employees, to reallocate work to remaining employees, and to train those survivors how to do the work they've absorbed--all of which eats managers' time and, therefore, money.

Other indirect costs include lost knowledge, skills, productivity, contacts, and customers, which are all hard to quantify, but are real factors in determining the short-term costs of laying people off. The ridiculous thing I've seen is that companies might make the balance sheet look good in the short term, but later have to hire people back.

Then What?

A company may lay off employees it considers the low end producers, but in doing so it creates a climate of personnel uncertainty. That uncertainty causes others to leave. One manager I know tells me that the first people to leave due to uncertainty in the company are the best people, because they can always get another job somewhere else.

In essence, the cost savings only last as long as the company doesn't need to rehire employees, and in most cases, that's not a long period of time. The employer will pay a premium price for attracting valuable replacements, including the cost of recruiting and screening candidates.

So does it really pay to layoff employees? At first glance layoffs seem to be an easy fix, but they don't appear to be a strategic initiative that pays off in the long run.

Chapter Seven: Motivation

Quote of the Week:

"Managers know how to do things right. Leaders know the right things to do."

Peter Drucker

Motivation is one of the key concepts for individuals for developing a professional work environment in every workplace. Depending on how motivated we are, determines the effort we put into our work and, therefore, determines how well we work, and if we will keep our jobs.

In short, without motivation, nothing gets done. Motivation is something that is approached differently by different organizations, but, ultimately, it is the responsibility of all immediate managers of staff.

Many state that employees will be motivated by money, while others believe money does not satisfy others (to a lasting degree). This supports the statement that human motivation is a personal characteristic, and not a one fits all option. I tend to believe you cannot motivate people – they must choose to be motivated. Without their choosing to be motivated, guns, lawyers, and money will not move them.

Managers who serve as leaders within the organization can help convey the right messages to engage employees and help them grow within their positions. Motivation can be increased through a number of ways—with incentives, feedback, recognition and rewards programs, and ensuring that the workplace meets basic needs and requirements for each employee. However, I have found that some shy away from public recognition, but crave it when given privately.

Let's view some challenges in the workplace. I think we are all motivated – to varying extents – to learn, grow, and achieve, but it takes compelling reasons for us to act.

Dear Dave:

I am wondering if you have done any articles comparing management types such as those who try to get employees to do more for the company by using praise and recognition or management that just uses threats and intimidation. I wish our management would learn how to develop better people skills, which in turn would make a job a lot more desirable.

A Reader

Dear Reader:

Managers as leaders tend to fall into 2 distinct camps: They either focus on tasks and productivity, or they focus on relationships and people. Scads of leadership studies bear this out. It really comes down to whether managers will try to change behaviors (task-oriented) or change attitudes (relationship-oriented).

I talked to one healthcare management employee who thinks change in any form needs to begin with a positive attitude. She says, "I believe that a positive attitude is imperative to provide motivation to change behavior.

Changing behaviors can be very difficult, but a manager's positive attitude and leadership skills will promote the best possible outcomes, and therefore support and encourage behavior changes."

Management theorist, McGregor, states there are 2 types of managers: Theory X and Theory Y. Without putting you to sleep (snore), let me explain what he believes and what can happen in organizations.

Theory X Managers do not trust employees and believe they are basically lazy.

Theory Y Managers believe employees can be trusted and will willingly work.

He goes on to say that there are also Theory X and Theory Y employees.

Theory X Employees cannot be trusted and will slack as much as they can.

Theory Y Employees can be trusted and want to work and contribute.

The mix of these managers and employees at work make for some very interesting – and very scary – relationships and motivation practices. Now, stay with me and I will try to make sense.

For instance: If you have a Theory X Manager managing a Theory X Employee you can well imagine the manager will be controlling and the employee just plain needs to be controlled. Things will not be optimal, but there may be short-term, positive results through management coercion and punishment.

Dave's note: Bad managers managing bad employees are not what you want.

However, if you have a Theory X Manager managing a Theory Y Employee, you will have a manager practicing control and mistrust when the employee really wants and deserves trust and the opportunity to contribute freely and productively. What will result is an employee that will learn to despise the manager and spend a great deal of time sending out resumes.

Now, think about a Theory Y Manager managing a Theory X Employee. The manager will start out trusting and supportive, but slowly and surely realize they need to lay down the law. Sadly, there is a chance these trusting managers may become cynical and start not trusting any employees. In essence, you just ruined a good manager because of bad employees.

Finally, consider a Theory Y Manager managing a Theory Y Employee. You have trustful managing the trustworthy. What a great arrangement. I believe most Theory X employees and Theory X managers can change. It will take education – lots of education... and maybe near death experiences.

So, as it does in so many cases, it comes down to hiring the best and the brightest managers and employees. Never skimp on the most critical part of your potential for success – the people.

Dave's Personal Nugget to a reader regarding people who just want to come to work, do their job, get paid, and never need any motivation.

Organizations tend to have 3 divisions of workers. The top 20% are stars and strive to add great value. The bottom 20% are those who will do as little as possible. You then have 60% of your workforce who really are the reliable workhorses doing good work every day.

Unfortunately, managers spend most if not all of their time developing the top talent and monitoring and disciplining the bottom feeders. The middle pack tends to get ignored and the managers may even forget these people are just people and fail to give them enough praise, recognition, and attention.

So, you hear managers say things like, "Those people are on auto-pilot and I don't need to worry about them." Well, the fact is they have self-esteem and also need or crave thank you's and recognition. If they were robots without personalities, only then would I agree with you that some people just need a paycheck.

Dear Dave,

I consider myself to be a good manager, but I feel like my employees are not that engaged in their work. It seems like they are just doing their work and have very little interest in what they are doing. How can I put some life back into these people? It's causing me to also lose interest in my job.

D

Dear D,

There is much you can do. You should be happy, though, that your people are at least doing their work – things could be worse.

Disengagement is Costly

We know that engaged and happy employees are a great asset for any business. However, new research has found that once engaged employees that have become disengaged can turn into a company's worst nightmare, because disengaged employees exhibit many negative and harmful behaviors at work.

Actively disengaged employees erode productivity while breaking the spirits of colleagues in the process. Conversely, involved and turned-on workers can create competitive advantage for the company by being more inspired in their work.

Disengaged employees must be motivated to perform on an hourly basis. They drag themselves through their day, contributing the bare minimum and often detracting from the work of their peers with negative comments or an overwhelming pessimism that is energy draining.

This pessimism is so toxic that it affects not only co-workers, but customers as well, driving away potential business and harming previously solid customer relationships. Research has shown that employee disengagement in the

United States adds up to approximately $350 billion dollars per year of lost productivity.

Reengaging the Disengaged

First, understand that getting employees turned-on isn't like flipping a switch – it may take time. I also believe that we cannot motivate people; they must choose to be motivated. All we can really do is make participation and involvement appear to be so valuable and enticing that employees choose to become engaged.

Creating and retaining engaged employees is heavily based on the style of management that a particular organization employs. However, while engaged employees are incredibly valuable to an organization, management must do its part to create an environment in which those individuals can thrive.

Actively encouraging people to contribute their ideas by creating an environment of trust, respect, and sharing, and by openly rewarding employees for those contributions, you will ultimately foster an environment which results in longer employee retention and an overall compelling atmosphere.

The research proves that those companies that do not provide a beneficial atmosphere ultimately hurt their own longevity and success. In that vein. Leaders must connect with their employees and show them they value them by congratulating them when praise and recognition are due.

Other Compelling Must Do's

Create a fundamentals checklist such as, ensuring the employee have the materials and equipment he or she needs to perform his or her job, and checking to see if the employee is clear about what is expected of him or her on a daily basis.

Also – and this is crucial—you must make sure that employees know what options are available for personal and professional development, but, in the short-term, make sure employees are experiencing challenging and meaningful work and are able to provide input about their work.

Above all else, show your employees that you value them and their contributions to the organization's success by acknowledging their efforts, showing them respect, and showing confidence in their abilities.

Dear Dave,

My company assumes that because we have a good product and service, and that our customers continue to buy our products, then we should be happy. We have lost good people and management is not doing enough to ensure the majority of employees don't leave. It seems like they train just enough, they offer just enough benefits, and they pay us enough to get by. I know I am just working the minimum to keep my job. Is this the right way to approach employee loyalty?

P

Dear P,

No, it is not a way for your company to motivate employees and keep their commitment. Employees truly committed to a common vision and motivated to go beyond their "normal" work is an awesome force.

I always teach my MBA students that employees are the most important resource your company has — treat your employees well and they will work hard and help make your business a success. However, your company – even if they believe that employees are extremely valuable – has developed a mindset of caring for the staff with the least amount of attention and rewards possible.

For the sake of argument, I wonder if your management realizes people may feel as you do. It could be they keep providing the minimum of development and rewards, because they have not heard complaints from staff nor seen sharp drops in productivity, sales, and effectiveness. In essence, they don't know what they are missing.

The Old Rule

In the old days – when yours truly was working his way up whatever the corporate ladder is—trust in corporations was achieved by the following: the employees were loyal; the company took care of the employees; employees had no other work priorities outside of the company; and the company developed, rewarded, and promoted employees who were eager to stay.

The Current (and future?) Rule

This is what I believe is happening today. The company tries to get good people; they try to provide interesting and challenging work, while trying to cut costs and keep their head above water; the employees are constantly looking for the best opportunities, while investing discretionary effort to produce as required, while carefully measuring what they are getting verses what they are putting in; and if the company and employees match their desires and expectations, work gets done, people stay, and – hopefully – the company stays in business.

Motivation 101

The days of the carrot and stick (rewards and punishment) style of management is not working and probably never really did. Management experts, such as Daniel Pink, believe companies must recognize and address the fact employees want...no, they crave, the deeply human need to direct their own lives, to learn and create new things, and to do better by themselves and the world. In essence, employees (and managers) want autonomy, mastery, and purpose.

Decay Amuck

Unfortunately, we – with or without knowing—have been chipping away at the basics of solid and effective work relationships and employee treatment for decades, if not centuries. Some managers believe, "You just can't trust those employees, because they are in it for themselves and will $%##@ you in a minute. Employees have come to believe, "You sure can't trust that company of mine...I will take care of myself, because no one else will." There it is! The beliefs have become the mentality, attitudes, and behavior.

Certainly, since the extensive layoffs of the last couple of years, this polarization of views has only increased. Can loyalty be restored? Yes, but, only if trust is restored. So, who moves first to restore loyalty? Managers? Employees? How about both managers and employees making great efforts to have and show concern not only for the job, but also for the mission of purpose, achievement, growth, and doing good work?

For You

What is your mission? What motivates you and makes you feel fulfilled? I will bet anything it is not doing the least possible and not taking pride in your abilities and contributions. One thing that has not changed is, the cream still rises to the top. A positive attitude and doing the best you can still get noticed. These things will help you achieve Pink's 3 motivators: autonomy, mastery, and purpose.

Dear Dave,

This is my first job after college. I came to this job with a lot of enthusiasm, I worked hard, and exceeding all the targets. I started aiming for promotion when I saw some of my coworkers being promoted. These people don't work harder or better than me and some just waste time. I have lost my interest and enthusiasm, so I decided to do enough to get by. I have been asked about my performance slow down and I just say I am very busy. Please help me, because I feel bad about this. I'm still performing better than the other workers, but I just hate being ignored or overlooked.

P

Dear P,

Be careful, because you are not going to prove anything by slowing down and reducing the quality of your work. In this tight job market it is wise to give it your all and be positive.

It is tough being a contributive, vital, and productive person in the workplace and be ignored and deprived of an opportunity to advance within the company.

We are all sensitive creatures that are aware of what is going on, who is getting what, and what we are not getting in comparison. In organizational behavior theory this is called Equity Theory, meaning we are constantly measuring what we are getting in comparison to others and, if we receive less than they get when doing the same amount and quality of work, we feel there is "inequity" and will do things to obtain equity – in your case, slowing down performance.

At least you aspire to still be promoted and, from what I can tell, still are motivated to perform well despite your observations and feelings. Many people simply *like* being ignored at work, so they can get away with a great deal, because no one notices.

One manager I know, who often hires people fresh out of college, tells me it's important for new entries in the workforce to know that if they are expecting to have instant credibility and recognition, they will not and it takes time, because there is a learning curve for both the new employee and management … and it needs patience.

For Managers

When you need to promote someone, which of your employees will you choose for that new or open supervisory position and what factors play into your choice?

Most managers will say they want loyalty, a dedicated work ethic, leadership and people skills, a positive, forward-thinking outlook and disposition, and the ability and desire to learn and improve.

If you can find an employee with all of these qualities, you are well on your way to lightening your load. This type of person will want to learn and grow and contribute, taking a huge weight off of you and your responsibilities.

For You

I really think it is best for you to be patient, stay professional and hard-working, and sit back and listen and learn. You will have much more credibility if you show that you are keeping your chin up and taking the time to see how things are done, while developing your skills and your ability to be a productive, contributing member of the organization.

In short, I advise you to stay positive – people dislike negative, antagonistic organizational parasites who could depress a clown convention. Managers (good ones) cannot trust and will not promote people who "play the system" and contribute less than expected or desired.

Make yourself a bit more helpful and indispensable to your boss and things will happen.

Dear Dave,

I am a mid-level manager and have been with my company for almost 20 years. I have seen so many changes in my company and the thing I really notice lately is employees seem to be just doing their job and they are not real excited about their work. I'm happy they work and do their job, but what can I do to get them enthused about what they do?

Signed,

Ron

Dear Ron,

Author, Marcus Buckingham, believes most employees are not engaged at work. He points to Gallup research that indicates that 54% of U.S. employees are not at all engaged at work and only 29% are truly motivated and engaged. Clearly, disengagement and unhappiness are recipes for lower productivity. "What is employee engagement?"

Many management gurus say engagement exists when employees feel empowered; they "own" their work and treat it as their business. They are proactive rather than reactive – they don't have to be told what to do. When engaged, workers are motivated in their work, excited about innovation and enthusiastic about continuous improvement.

Business writer, Mark Bowman believes if three critical strategies were applied, we might see a turn-around in these sorry workplace statistics.

These three strategies are...

1. Proper placement and use of talent in specific jobs (to include further developing those talents),

2. Appropriate accountability and incentives,

3. Accurate performance appraisal.

Try to work on these three. Of course, depending on circumstances, there are other issues that help as well, such as loyalty and congeniality.

Dear Dave,

Our company is trying to develop a plan to compensate our sales staff. Some say commission only pay structures motivate salespeople, and others claim that the pay structure should be a salary arrangement so the sales people are able to survive in lean times. Do you have any thoughts on this?

Mike

Dear Mike,

Sales management experts believe people feel secure with set incomes. However, it is also believed that sales people produce more and take better care of their customers if there is a commission "carrot" that makes them try a little harder.

In view of this, I vote for a package that provides a reasonable guaranteed dollar amount and also provides an opportunity to make more through incentive structures such as:

- o a commission based on a percentage of gross revenues or gross margin
- o incentives paid when sales targets are attained, or
- o contests that are extremely attractive to the sales people.

You could also consider an incentive arrangement that will pay the salesperson's expenses if targets are hit. Commissions can also be paid for other goals such as opening new accounts, merchandising and account management targets, and success stories of service excellence.

Dear Dave,

At my company, tough economic times have caused a reduction in raises and benefits. Would you be able to let us know other ways managers can make their employees feel valued without financial rewards? Also, are there tips on how the rewards can be given to make them feel extra sincere?

M

Dear M,

Leadership experts say the single greatest need people have is to be appreciated. Accordingly, employee motivation and performance management depend on good rewards (appreciation) systems.

People think that money is a motivator. It does have an effect, but motivation involves far more. A good rewards system recognizes and rewards individual and team performance, financially and otherwise, in relation to the overall contribution made.

The best performance appraisal system in the world will not work if it is linked to rewards that employees do not trust or support. In short, a motivated employee will achieve a great deal. A demotivated employee will be slow, prone to error, and not likely to achieve targeted results.

There are many nonfinancial ways to reward employees. Before you reward an employee it is beneficial to find out what kinds of rewards act as incentives for that employee or group of employees. People are different and value different things. For example, some employees may respond well to recognition of achievement before their peers, while others may find that embarrassing.

One of my business colleagues believes employees are more likely to be motivated to improve their performance through the use of nonmonetary rewards such as being thanked publicly at a departmental function, having lunch with the head of the organization, or receiving an extra day off.

Flexibility is a mantra businesses must embrace and is increasingly important in keeping and motivating employees (and managers). Flexibility takes many forms including flex-time, work-at-home schedules, job sharing, and comp time.

Empowerment is craved by most employees. It is when power or authority is given to employees so they can make even small decisions regarding their working life. For instance, workers have control over how to use their time and deciding the priority of tasks that need to be done.

Education is another way to keep employees productive and happy. This education can be formal or informal, but the more systematic it is, the better.

When everyone has worked hard to complete a project, throw a little party or take everyone to lunch. There are endless inexpensive ways to recognize people's value including the simple thank you in the hall.

More important, though, is your internal communication. People who understand the "what and the why" things need to be accomplished generally work harder to achieve objectives.

There are ways you can express interest in their personal well-being. You can seek their advice, help them to develop opportunities for advancement, facilitate family leave, and most importantly, you can show empathy and understanding for his or her particular situation without showing favoritism.

In summary, companies must institute compensation and rewards systems that fairly treat and recognize all employees, regardless of their level within the organization. This involves matching rewards with the contribution made, particularly where job requirements can change rapidly.

Dear Dave,

I attended a company training last week focusing on customer satisfaction. The trainer briefly talked about employees and said the employee experience should be as enjoyable and engaging as the customer experience. As a manager, I want to know more about how to enhance the employee experience. Besides good pay and benefits, rewarding work, and good management, what else adds to this ideal experience?

P

Dear P,

The short answer is you must first understand your employees, their struggles, their frustrations and their needs, and their wants and desires, and then build an environment that enables and encourages thinking, contribution, and action.

Your employees have beliefs they bring to the company – often baggage, such as bad experiences with past employment and management – and these beliefs fuel the employee to either be vibrant, engaged, active, and contributing, or, skeptical, cynical, negative, and disengaged.

In many cases, employees show up and do their work, but there is low commitment, pride, and enthusiasm. You can see that "thousand yard stare" in their eyes and that, they would rather be anywhere but at work.

Think about yourself as a guide for understanding. What do you really care about? What engages you? How do you know when you are on fire versus just going through the paces? When do you feel exhilarated, deeply involved, and interested and like you are really doing great things that matter?

The "Promise" is the Experience

Envision what "the experience" should be for employees. Imagine what it would feel like – as one of your employees — to want to come into work, spring into action, feel turned-on and really feel interested in your work, the well-being of the team, and seeing the company prosper. Ask other managers for their views.

What is "the company promise" to employees? I hope there is one, other than just making money. If you could write "the ideal promise," who should hear "the promise," what exactly is it, and what would it feel like to experience "the promise" lived and shared?

Investigate

Assess the current experience employees have. Observe them at work. Talk to them. Ask them sincere questions about their work experience and how they try to find balance in their lives. Ask what you could do to help them do their job better.

One long-time businessperson I know empowers his employees to help them find meaning. He says, "I ask each employee to come up with 3 ideas that will help the business. We discuss the ideas openly. The employees are then asked to do some research and figure out a way to implement their idea. It works quite well and they become very motivated."

I believe you should ask employees about what makes the company different, interesting or valuable. Find out how they describe the culture, vision, and characteristics of the company. Where are the "moments of truth" where they, their team, and the company are, or are not, at its best?

What you are really looking for is, whether or not, the employees have perceptions of pride, enthusiasm, emotional attachment, and a sense they are part of something big, rather than just functioning as burnt-out robots.

Build and Act

Now the rubber meets the road. Being armed with all of this knowledge, decide how you can assist employees understand and appreciate what you believe and how great it would be to be turned-on, engaged, and enthused about their contributions.

Lead the way through your modeling and displaying a winning attitude and pride in your work. Nothing sells better than success. Show your strength when dealing with adversity and not letting it get you down. Remember, a spiraling, downhill stream of negativity and doom is contagious ... and usually starts with management.

Lead the way through helping employees see and embrace how their roles, their functions, their inputs, ideas, thinking, and suggestions help the company deliver "the promise."

Lead the way by helping your employees and fellow managers become more engaged, positive, and solution-minded versus just waiting around for problems to occur and then running around shouting, "We're all going to die!"

Finally, lead the way by engaging senior management in the conversation and plan. Ask them for guidance to ensure that managers have both the tools and the skills to inspire engaged and committed employees.

Dear Dave,

As a manager I have a pretty good group of people, who work hard and are productive. These folks are reliable and attendance is not a problem, except for one individual. This worker really is a good worker when she is present, but in the last several months she has missed work coming up with every excuse under the sun. I don't want to fire her, but she is affecting our work environment. Ideas?

M

Dear M,

It's a fact that if you have a job, you need to be in the office to complete your work. Generally speaking, if you are hired by a company and are an employee for them, you need to be in the office every day. A big part of being a professional is being a reliable worker.

I realize that no matter what your job we all need a mental health day away from work every once in a while. However, some people seem to have a grandma that dies every couple of weeks.

Whether your employee likes it or not, this is her job. Her coworkers count on her to be there to do her work every day. If she isn't reliable and misses countless days of work, then it's likely that her coworkers, or you, will have to pick up your slack. This can breed resentment and anger.

Absence Amuck

There are all sorts excuses and reasons employees miss a day of work. The real issue takes place when they start misusing sick days and take too much time off. If this is something your employee is doing, it had better be addressed right away. Her reasons for being out frequently don't matter. What matters is the end result — the fact that she isn't reliably at work.

Spotty attendance might signal any of a range of issues, from a problem at home or job dissatisfaction. Talk with your employee privately to find out if she has encountered a difficult personal problem, such as a relationship breakup or an ill family member.

However, if your discussion reveals dissatisfaction with her job, perhaps the employee needs to consider adjusting her attitude, or if the job is a good fit for her. You may have to remind her that chronic and unexplained absences will be treated according to your company's written attendance disciplinary policy.

It's difficult deciding whose excuses are legitimate and whose aren't, but, it is your job is to ensure that you have a reliably present workforce. — and right now, you have a problem child and her behavior could become contagious.

What to Do

Tell her she has been missing work and you need to be able to count on her to be there reliably, and while you certainly understand that things come up from time to time, the frequency of these unplanned absences is too high. Mention, going forward, I need you to be here reliably, every day, except in the most extreme of circumstances. Ask her to commit to doing that.

From there, stick to it. If she continues to have unplanned absences at a rate that you find unacceptable, you need to enforce consequences. However, if this is a long-term employee whose work has always been good and this is a recent problem, you should express concern and ask what's going on, and try to solve the problem.

Dear Dave,

I manage several people and almost all of them are motivated and work hard. My problem is, I have two workers who are extremely talented with good education and experience, but they are very unmotivated doing as little as possible to get by. What can I do to get these high-potential workers to become more motivated?

C

Dear C,

For the employer, talented people pose both an opportunity and a risk. What gives talent its potential also makes it either impatient or apathetic. In short, being motivated is a choice we make no matter how much talent we possess.

Highly talented people have very different values and motivation from the majority of people. More is expected of them and they often expect more in return. They are often high-impact, but can be high-maintenance too.

Any manager (including my manager colleagues) will tell you talented workers think differently (and faster) — but they get bored more readily. They can deal with more complexity but are more complex in themselves, because hey get frustrated more readily.

What Turns Them On

A recent *McKinsey Quarterly* survey found respondents view three noncash motivators — praise from immediate managers, leadership attention (for example, one-on-one conversations), and a chance to lead projects or task forces are even more effective motivators than the three highest-rated financial incentives: bonuses, increased pay, and stock options.

The survey's top three nonfinancial motivators play critical roles in making employees feel that their companies value them, take their well-being seriously, and strive to create opportunities for career growth.

In another study, the following factors are ranked as to how essential they were to keeping talented people motivated:

    o Values and culture in the company. 58%

- o Freedom and autonomy to do the job. 56%
- o The job has exciting challenges. 51%
- o They are well managed. 50%

These findings tell us that employees – who we consider highly-talented or even "average workers" – want more purpose and engagement from their work, their management, and their work environment.

Money is Not a Motivator

Money alone doesn't motivate talented people. And, unfortunately, money is how we rate everyone. How much do they earn? This can be as much about ego as money, but just because you can exploit certain talented people doesn't mean you should.

They (talented employees) take pride in being good at what they do, and they want to be paid equitably. However, even though it appears that talented employees want ample compensation for what they do, what they really desire is purpose, achievement, and management that doesn't ride them like a rented mule.

What Else is Needed?

Talented people thrive on challenge and become frustrated when forced to endure routine, meaningless, or boring tasks. They are a different kind of person—and they need a different kind of management. Also, the manager must be respected.

Seek out their input and encourage participation. Encourage fun—generally, we enjoy doing what we do well and do well what we enjoy doing. One cannot achieve one's full potential doing things that one does not enjoy.

Think in terms of removing obstacles in front of them so that they can use their talent to stay on mission rather than dissipate it dealing with issues of politics, environment, compensation, and appropriate recognition.

But, let me be clear: If you have done all you can to help these people become motivated and they are making no progress – and especially if they are negatively affecting the output and well-being of their coworkers—I don't care how talented they are ... replace them.

Chapter Eight: Stress

Workplace stress is the harmful physical and emotional response that occurs when there is a poor match between job demands and the capabilities, resources, or needs of the worker. That's the text book definition, but I believe what I was told by the mother of my sister-0in-law at a family picnic, "We just get damn tired!"

A variety of factors contribute to workplace stress such as too much work, extensive hours worked, toxic work environments, lack of autonomy, difficult relationships among coworkers and management—management bullying, harassment, and lack of opportunities or motivation to advancement in one's skill level.

Some stress is normal. In fact, it is often what provides us with the energy and motivation to meet our daily challenges both at home and at the workplace. Stress in these situations is the kind that helps you "rise" to a challenge and meet your goals such as deadlines, sales or production targets, or finding new clients.

However, we are reduced to nervous wrecks because of burnout, fatigue, torturous pressure to produce, and ridden like a rented mule, one can hardly say that stress is productive. In fact, it has to be right up there with hate for your immediate boss as the leading cause of quitting a job.

I believe employers - it is their responsibility—should assess the workplace for the risk of stress and help employees deal with it. In the following situations I will do what employers should be doing - helping people deal with stress.

Dear Dave

The stress in my company is so bad, the employees are constantly unhappy and we lose good people all of the time. I am almost afraid to attend meetings or open my e-mail, because all I ever see is somebody telling me how poorly we are doing our jobs and threatening us that we will be terminated if things don't change. I am feeling physically ill, my attitude is bad, and I hate to go to work. I have to admit that we do get paid fairly well and that is the only reason I and everybody else stays with the company. How can I cope and manage my health and attitude? Is there anything that I can do as just one employee to change this dreadful situation?

Signed: Pins and Needles

Dear Pins,

Your company has obviously adopted a management structure that is all too common in so many American organizations that believe constant pressure, micro-managing and inducing fear is the best way to get things done. You are on pins and needles because you are working for – dare I say it – "pricks." Sorry for that attempt at humor.

Your management has never learned how to lead, but they did learn from others how to smother and threaten people, and believe this is the best way to manage. I wish I had a button to push that would remove these people from their positions and reassign them to picking up litter on Bolivian highways, but we must learn to deal with them and not let them destroy our health and happiness.

First, let's look at why people manage that way. The first and most obvious reason is they probably have poor self-esteem, no leadership skills, and the inability to trust others. This compels them to ride people like rented mules, simply because they just cannot delegate responsibility, and they do not trust others will do their jobs without constantly applying threats, intimidation, or coercion.

A fundamental belief in organizational development theory is people innately crave to learn and apply their skills, and many organizations are not designed to allow this to happen. This means people come to organizations totally willing to grow, produce, and help the organization succeed, but are slapped-down, ignored, insulted, or embarrassed every time they try to do these things. Finally, they just give up and try to work within the confines of the structure that exists and realize communication, feedback, and ideas are not welcomed, nor encouraged.

What you can do and your options are:
- o Quit and find a company that believes and trusts their employees.
- o Learn to cope, swallow your pride, and just do your job and collect your paycheck.
- o Stay positive and constructive, while helping others control their fears and emotions.

Dave votes for option number three. If you do stay positive, constructive, and try your best to be productive despite the culture that exists, these acts will actually help you cope and feel better about yourself and your ability to not let others get you down. This attitude becomes a very reinforcing system – not to mention contagious—that will help you maintain your own self-esteem and pride.

You will actually feel stronger by trying your best to be stronger. This positive attitude will actually become a contagious and inspiring form of leadership that helps others feel stronger and able to cope with the adversity. Others will covet to have what you have.

If you spread gloom and doom, then gloom and doom becomes the climate. If you show others that you can weather the management structure, your own self-respect will grow and others will try to learn what you are doing. Also, the management weasels in your company will tend to leave you alone, because they think you got the message and are not a problem.

Plan B would be to vocalize your concerns and try to change the management system and culture that exists. This is a courageous and often deadly route to travel, but if you sense you can make a difference and feel you must be heard, then diplomatically, methodically, and persuasively plan how you want to communicate your message.

This "Plan B" is fondly named "life is too short and I am mad as (expletive) and I cannot take this anymore" theory. This plan assumes you are ready to face the potential repercussions you may experience from management who state: "Well...We got a problem with this worker. Now what do we do?"

There is a chance managers may see the wisdom of your message and try to create a culture that is less threatening and more inspiring. However, there is a chance they just plain like this form of management and will do everything in their power to show you the door.

My suggestion: Try to stay positive, constructive, and stable while helping managers see the ills of their ways the best you can. Or make sure your computer is working soundly, so you can search and apply for job opportunities.

I firmly believe we cannot stand idly by and watch this inept, damaging form of management go unchecked or unaddressed. We have to maintain our physical and mental health and reach out to help others with the same.

Dear Dave,

Do all companies these days expect those who are able to constantly pick up the slack of inferior personnel to save labor hours with no appreciable reward for doing so, other than the right to keep your job? My co-workers and I feel underappreciated.

Worked to Death

Dear Worked,

First, let me say you should be happy you have a job. Economists report the recession is over (on paper), but try telling that to the millions without jobs.

The reasons employees are doing extra work these days are not what you may think. Roughly 72% of employees across the country report that they work through lunch, while 70% report working beyond scheduled time and on weekends, according to the new "Pressure to Work: The Employees' Perspective" poll released by the Society for Human Resource Management (SHRM).

The SHRM poll reports more than half (52%) of polled employees admit that "self-imposed pressure" is the main reason for working beyond scheduled time. Only one in five polled employees (21%) cite "pressure from immediate supervisor/manager" as the reason for working extra hours. Even fewer (12%) cite "pressure from top management" as a source of pressure.

One manager I know believes employees will feel more appreciated if management communicates how individual contributions will help the department and the company to succeed. He says that managers must establish clear goal and objectives for employees that can be measured, are tied to a specific time frame, and are realistic.

If employees see how their day to day work is a part of the bigger picture and how the goals are tied to the company strategy, they will become more engaged and not see themselves exploited or forced to do more.

This means, of course, managers should provide performance updates and recognition to those who are delivering results, while also addressing those employees whose contributions are low or declining."

Now, are there some employers that will take advantage of the economic crisis, work their employees like rented mules, and make their employees do extra work and work extra hours because they know employees have few options to resist or seek work elsewhere? Yes. However, remember, almost all employers are trying everything they can to stay afloat and need their valuable employees to help in any way they can.

The problem may not be the extra work employees are taking on, but, rather, that the employer is not clearly communicating the reasons and purpose for the extra work to the employees. I believe employees will pitch in and do what is needed if they clearly know why and are treated with consideration and respect.

This means employers must get employees more involved in the needs and goals of the company. Managers must inspire employees and help them see themselves as valuable and appreciated contributors to the survival of the company.

Dear Dave,

I am bored and burned out with my job. I feel like I am not getting anywhere and I know there is not any growth potential in the job I am doing. My coworkers tell me my feelings will pass and I shouldn't be frustrated and stressed. I know I have more to offer than what I am doing. Advice?

K

Dear K,

There is not a one of us who does not feel the way you do from time to time. I know many people who love their work and where they work, but still get fried every so often and think they would rather be digging ditches in a swamp.

I've got to first say this – as I always do – be happy you have a job. Also, I will warn you that your emotions and feelings may be showing and managers pick up on this stuff – you don't want to lose your job.

Burnout Defined

Burnout is a state of emotional, mental, and physical exhaustion caused by excessive and prolonged stress. It occurs when you feel overwhelmed and unable to meet constant demands. As the stress continues, you begin to lose the interest or motivation that led you to take on a certain role in the first place.

However, burnout also occurs when people are bored out of their mind and they are doing nothing more than going through the motions at work. I guess you could say that boredom is a lack of stress that causes stress.

When you're burned out, problems seem insurmountable, everything looks bleak, and it's difficult to muster up the energy to care—let alone do something about your situation. When everything looks like the sing-song, repetitive, unchallenging same-old same-old, you check out and feel under-employed and unmotivated.

While you're usually aware of being under a lot of stress, you don't always notice burnout when it happens. And, it affects your home and personal life, too, because you carry it around with you.

What Now?

You need to find a way to get and stay energized. Obviously, you need challenge in your life and it appears you may need a different job or more responsibilities in your job, too. The quickest and best solution to boredom is activity, and the greatest cure for a lack of caring is to find something to care about and some reason to care.

No one is going to be standing next to you all day with pom poms and a megaphone shouting Tony Robbins "motivational rants" at you all day – plus, who in the heck would want that?

As a management colleague puts it, "you need to live your way into a new way of thinking instead of thinking your way into a new way of living." This means … get busy and do something about your situation.

Start preparing for a new job or career, while keeping your chin up and staying positive in the job you have. There are many schools offering degrees, training, and career paths. Check them out. I know education costs money, but it is a wonderful investment.

Finally, beyond your job, take up some new interests that you can look forward to each day. Hobbies, clubs, volunteerism, and projects allow you a chance to stay busy and feel productive – plus, they allow you to network with folks who just may have knowledge of a career move for you (wink wink).

Dear Dave,

Our company has eliminated jobs, and I now have more work than I can handle. How can I ask for help in a way that doesn't make me look inadequate or incompetent? My coworkers tell me to not say anything, because I may look like a weak player.

R

Dear R,

You are not alone—many people working today feel overloaded. For some reason, most people – especially successful ones—think that asking for help is a sign of weakness, when, in fact, it just makes sense.

If you have identified that you are not speaking up about something you need help with, let me give you some free advice: Ask for help! All your personal reasons for not asking for help could create severe errors.

However, before you ask for help you have to do the research to make sure you can't do the work yourself and that you actually need help. Take a hard look at your workload to make sure it is truly overwhelming and determine if maybe you are actually burnt or stressed out.

Organizing Your Work

You acknowledge that you have acquired more responsibility, but maybe you could use some help in judging what tasks need to be done first and which ones can wait.

Before talking to your boss, carefully gain an objective picture of your situation. Determine (triage) which activities are critical, what can be dropped, and whether some work can wait. Prioritizing work will also help you decide if there are any activities you are doing more for your own satisfaction than for meeting organizational needs.

It is possible that your problem is inefficiency. Determine if constant distractions—whether from people, e-mail, Facebook updates or even day-dreaming—might be why you aren't meeting your obligations. It might be that it takes you an hour to settle into work in the morning.

After assessing your work disruptors, you can tackle them by trying to stop the interruptions or getting down to work faster. Please know that I'm not suggesting that you are sloppy about getting down to work, I am just stating it can happen to anyone and we may not realize it.

Don't Complain

No one likes complainers: you risk negative fallout only if you complain to your boss that you can't handle your job. Don't go up to him or her complaining, "I have too much work," because your boss probably has too much work, too.

Be proactive and try to offer some solutions when you ask for support. If you're struggling, admit it promptly, otherwise you're liable to miss deadlines and compromise your performance, not to mention your job. Be specific and show that you've thought about why the situation has arisen and set some targets.

Coworkers Can Help

I sense you have a collaborative relationship with your co-workers, and maybe you can ask if they can help you with certain tasks. But generally it's better to go through your manager, because it's possible co-workers may be busier than they seem.

But, remember, you have to put in your full effort, otherwise people aren't going to want to help you. People are amazing and willing to lend a hand if they know you truly tried your best and still need their help.

Asking for help can show strength rather than weakness and shows you have the company's best interests at heart.

Chapter Nine: Decision Making

Decisions are at the heart of success, and at times there are critical moments when they can be difficult, perplexing, and nerve racking. Also, don't forget the fact that not all decisions lead to great outcomes.

Decisions are educated guesses to a large extent. Companies have been brought down because of bad decisions that may or may not have been made using a great deal of data and information. Although it is wise to accumulate all of the facts and evidence you can before deciding, the truth is, there may not always be a great deal to go on and we need to act fast.

For whatever reasons and with whatever methods we use to make decisions, in business, decisions are often tough to make. So, we may rely on gut feel" for choosing, because something "feels right" or we have seen such and such before. The fallacy is, things change and what was right and made sense 3 months ago may not hold any merit whatsoever today as evidence for decision making.

CEOs are paid zillions of dollars because they can make the best and biggest decisions. We pay them big time, because they have been there and done that, so they must be right. Right? Wrong. Even they are subject to personal bias, using shortcuts and rules of thumb, or choosing without having supports for their choices.

In the everyday workplace, we make choices all day long. In fact, we can choose to not even show up for work – then we would need to choose transportation to the unemployment office. We can choose who we associate with and talk to. We can choose how we react to things, or plan, or do the work we have to do.

So aside from all that, we see that making the correct decisions is not only what we want to do, but includes what we have to do. We all know the difference between "right" and "wrong," and we can tell "good from "bad." But we also know that the more difficult decisions come when we have to choose between good and better. The toughest decisions of all are those we have to make between bad and worse.

Checkout my responses to some decision problems. You can make a decision of whether or not I know what I am talking about.

Dear Dave,

I work for a busy department in a company and my problem is with my team of employees. We get along really well and almost never have any conflicts that we cannot solve. Our problem is we cannot make decisions and everything is put off. This is so frustrating, because we need to decide on things so we can move on. Any suggestions?

K

Dear K,

I can't decide what to tell you. Sorry. Bad pun.

On a recent Harvard Business Review's Answer Exchange a list of the biggest problems that teams encounter includes the inability to make decisions. I call it "Decidius Nervosa"

I'm not so sure—according to my wife—that I'm the best person to offer anyone sound advice regarding decision making, but I do think it is an issue that each of us is faced with on a daily basis throughout our lifetimes and most often at work. When individuals on a team have difficulty making a decision, trust me, the whole team will follow suit.

Team Realities

Management text books define group or team decision making as a type of participatory process in which multiple individuals acting collectively, analyze problems or situations, consider and evaluate alternative courses of action, and select from among the alternatives a solution or solutions. Whew! That sounds nice and orderly.

That is the text book view. However, reality teaches us that feelings of dread will build inside team members simply by the mere thought of making a change. At other times it may be neither the thought of change, nor even the challenge that research and thinking must be involved in the process of deciding; it is the inability to accept the fact that they (the team) must stand by what was decided. That is commitment and commitment is so committal.

Would you be able to work with the other extreme? – people who leap without looking, figuring that all will go well and getting more data and information to make an intelligent decision is too messy and time-consuming. This decision style will get themselves in sticky predicaments quite often and quickly.

Also, not all decisions carry the same weight of potential impact. Some decisions are a simple matter of whether to make a change or not, while others may involve restructuring, large investments of money, great effort, and substantial time investments.

Sometimes you cannot blame the team for the inability to feel confident in making a decision, because there may be important factors and constraints afoot including unclear goals, different interpretations, incorrect information, or even the very fact the team just plain does not get along.

What To Do

Decision-making is more natural to certain personalities. If there are people on your team that can make decisions, these people should focus on improving the quality of team decisions and assist the undecided "nervous Nellies."

I believe that if a team can select a decision making method that is embraced and used routinely, the more comfortable team members will be with making decisions that stick. The methods to make decisions are not rocket surgery and the following is a rudimentary and very usable model:

Define and clarify the issue — does it warrant action? If so, when? Is the matter urgent, important, or both.

1. Gather all the facts and understand their causes.

2. Think about, or brainstorm, possible options and solutions

3. Consider and compare the pros and cons of each option — consult outside the team if needed for an objective perspective.

4. Select the best option — avoid vagueness and be specific.

Explain your decision to those involved and affected, and follow up (measure) to ensure proper and effective implementation.

I have always believed that consensus is overrated. I believe in getting down in the mud and slugging it out, and challenging each other to think, defend their logic, reasoning, and beliefs, and really approach and come close to that rarity in business called *dialogue*. Accordingly, dissent is a good sign and shows the team is thinking.

My financial advisor, Ray, has a sign in his office, "If everyone is thinking alike, then no one is really thinking." Quite possibly, a team demonstrating diversity of thought and perspectives may actually assist the team members to come to agreed-upon conclusions and, "Voila," making real and binding decisions.

Chapter Ten: Innovation

Innovation is not just about ideas; it is the successful implementation of ideas that lead to more value for whatever business you are in. Sounds simple, eh? No, innovation must become a consistent capability and core discipline in order to compete in an exceptionally fast moving and competitive marketplace. And to do this, the ideas of the employees must be heard.

Check out the ideas of others. I'm not saying you need to spend a great deal of time and money on every idea that surfaces, but take the time to glean what you see and hear and find out if something proposed might just make sense. To be clear, an idea—as creative as it may be – cannot be called an "innovation" until it is implemented ... meaning made actionable as an applied improvement of some kind.

I have found over the years that the best ideas come from the people closest to the tasks – the people who are in the trenches and deal head-on with the things that make the business tick. These are frontlines people who see and discuss this or that which may fertile ground for improvement. These are the people who deal with both happy and angry customers. These are the folks who are responsible for their piece of work to fit the whole of whatever the company offers. I think you get my point.

Why is it, then, that we gather often-detached members of an organization to talk about and plan innovation when these folks may have last visited the production floor or talked to a customer once in the last blue moon. Accordingly, why don't we gather in the people who see what goes right and goes wrong and ask them what they think? For that matter, why aren't customers made as close as white on rice, so you can hear what they think before coming out with 38 new colors and sizes of a defective product?

The best ideas come from those who work with the core pieces of the business. These folks are the eyes and ears of the functions and workings of what will make or break the company. Let's read about innovation and hear from some folks who are close or light years away from what should or could be improved.

Dave's Nugget for Management

The authors of *Managing and Organizations* came up with a list of **10 ways managers can kill creativity at work.** Here are a few of them:

Never talk to employees on a personal level, except for annual meetings – at which you praise your leadership skills.

Create boundaries between decision-makers, technical staff, and creative minds. Make sure that they can't talk to each other.

Make sure that creative people do a lot of technical and detailed work, such as counting things.

Be highly critical (they love it!) and withhold positive feedback, which would only encourage them to do things.

Police your employees by every procedural means that you can devise. Insist that they stick to the rules of good old bureaucracy and fill in many forms – lots of forms.

Dear Dave,

At my work, all I hear is that we should be innovative. It seems to me what our management is really telling us is to cut costs. What do they want from us and what do they really

mean? Where are innovative opportunities found in any company?

Signed,

Barb

Dear Barb,

You are asking the business question of the decade and possibly the century, because organizational leaders know that innovation is essential to keeping the company alive and attain superior competitive advantage. Typically, business innovation focuses on improving quality, reliability, and safety.

Let's start with defining the word, innovation. Historically, innovation means the introduction of new things or methods. The term is most used these days as to improve on something that exists, such as a product or process. Thus, business leaders want all employees thinking about new and better ways to satisfy customers and simplify and improve things.

In order to innovate, you must think and in order to think, you must know where you are at and what you have. Far be it from me to answer questions only with more questions, but consider these questions that may open up your eyes to improvement areas:

- o What are our company's shortcomings? Are they something that can't be ignored?
- o How do we communicate? Do we? How can we communicate better?
- o Are there any processes we use every day that can be improved?
- o Are there ways we can solve problems better?
- o How can we enhance the emotional experience for our customers?

One manager I know says, "Creating a culture hungry to find new and innovative ways to be competitive requires management to have a clear mission, but also to give the team freedom to try things that may fail. Teams that feel ownership of the issues as well as the success of the company are more likely to find solutions for the changing environment."

In summary, you don't need to be designing complex products or changing the whole company to be innovative. Innovation can be simple. I am sure there are things that nag at you at work and should be improved; start with those.

Dear Dave,

As a manager, I truly value the ideas and suggestions of my employees. Over the years, our company has saved money, become more efficient, and has become a better place to work, because of the great ideas from employees. If employee feedback and input is so valuable, why do so many employees from other companies tell me they are never heard or even asked if they have ideas?

P

Dear P,

First, let me say that I applaud you for being a manager who listens to employees and tries to capitalize on their creativity. Second – as I always do – I have a lot to say about valuing the thinking of employees and why, often times, their ideas are never considered.

It's a virtuous circle: Workers become more engaged when they see their ideas being used. And managers, seeing the impact of employees' ideas, give employees more authority – which leads to more and better ideas. It's not rocket surgery!

Squashed Like a June Bug

Good managers know frontline workers have better knowledge of the particularities of products, services, and processes than managers do. These employees are close to the work and they're better positioned to spot problems and opportunities.

124

What often happens is, management will proudly state, "We want employee ideas, creativity, suggestions, and problem solving (harumph, yada yada)!" Then, everyone feels happy and thinks the company is great and truly cares about them as contributive, thinking people.

But, here is the clincher: The employees then see things that may be wrong, or can be improved, and come up with ideas. They then proudly go tell their manager about what they came up with and they hear something like this, "We kinda like the way things are, but, thank you very much." Worse, they may hear, "You're paid to work and not to think!"

Then, the employees go back to their work, somewhat disheartened, a bit hurt, but most certainly convinced this whole spiel about using our ideas was a bogus, "feel good" sham. Employees talk to each other – yes, they do – and the talk becomes, "That's the last time I'll suggest anything."

One local healthcare professional I know believes management sets the example. He states, "Employees find it disingenuous when organizations solicit ideas and don't implement them into practice. The inability of senior managers to "walk—the-talk," has been linked with employee dissatisfaction, poor performance and increase in turnover rate."

The Idea System

Most employees have lots of ideas and would be thrilled to see them used. They don't want to see their company go down the tube, so they take pride in contributing to the organization's success. So, the most effective form of idea recognition is to implement their ideas and to give credit to the employees involved.

Submitting ideas should be simple, and the evaluation of suggestions should be quick and effective. Pushing decision making down to the front lines for as many ideas as possible leads to better decisions, faster implementation, and lower processing costs; it also frees up managers' time.

All businesses need to be looking for ways to cut costs, improve customer service, and drive performance. It's a jungle out there. Capturing employee suggestions and ideas engages and improves employee motivation, creating a more productive and satisfying work environment. Employee participation breeds buy-in and engagement.

For Managers

Managers can make idea submission part of their meetings, employee reviews, or simply in every-day conversations with employees by asking them what they see going on, what nagging problems or improvement opportunities they see, and if they have any ideas for improvement.

Believe it or not, employees can think and have a lot to say. By being open and receptive to ideas, you allow everyone to get involved and thereby create a receptive atmosphere and culture for change, innovation, and continuous improvement.

The more people you gather ideas from, the more likelihood of finding the most creative solutions. Also, ongoing, meaningful rewards and recognition for ideas that are used provide an effective, low cost way of raising morale and encouraging higher levels of performance.

Dear Dave,

My company is always talking about creativity and innovation. They expect all employees to be creative, especially those who want to become managers. Well, I'm just not creative and I have tried. I like to know what work I need to do and do it. This fact may hold me back. What can I do?

T

Dear T,

You've just show creativity by writing to me with a question. How does that feel? Now, I will try to provide you a creative, but realistic answer.

There are many things you can do to enhance your creativity ... or, as you put it, lack of creativity. Like anything, we can learn to be more creative – it is not just a skill for select people. However, we often will label people as "creative types" when they are just trying new ways to look at things.

Many people see creativity as a mysterious, magical process where one moment there is nothing and the next moment ... brilliance! That is simply not the case. Creativity is not magic, it is a skill that can be learned with a little effort and thinking.

Creativity is all about finding new ways of solving problems and approaching situations. This isn't a skill restricted to artists, musicians, or writers; it is a useful skill for people from all walks of life. If you've ever wanted to boost your creativity, there are things you can do.

Creating Creativity

I like to self-brainstorm ideas. Brainstorming is a common technique in both academic and professional settings, but it can also be a powerful tool for developing your creativity.

Start by suspending your judgment and self-criticism, then start writing down related ideas and possible solutions for a challenge. The goal is to generate as many ideas as possible in a relatively short span of time. Next, focus on clarifying and refining your ideas in order to arrive at the best possible choice.

One of my professor colleagues says, "Creativity comes from the exchange of ideas driven by asking powerful questions. The thinking of two or more individuals in solving a problem will yield better results than the ideas of just one."

In a similar fashion, departed Steven Jobs argued that the best inventors seek out "diverse experiences, collecting lots of dots that they later link together. Instead of developing a narrow specialization. I, myself, always try to experience new things and talk to people I would not normally talk to … and try not to bug them.

Creative people do not dream up massive ideas or schemes out of thin air. Creativity is a process of baby steps that tip-toes from small idea to small idea. Over time, the build up of these numerous small ideas creates a large and powerful idea.

Make time to develop your ideas. Try to schedule a regular time when you can be alone with your thoughts. Take a walk in the afternoon. I, personally, prefer the peace and quiet of the early morning before I become busy.

Day dream – go ahead, it won't hurt you. Make time so that your mind can wander and look for relationships and intersections of things that seem to be unrelated. Inventions and innovations come from combinations of different things.

No idea is too small or too big. Write them down and follow where they lead you. Don't let reason or insecurity squash any potentially creative thoughts, because – heaven forbid – we don't want others to think we are weird.

Chapter Eleven:
Persuasion

As Plato observed, persuasion is the key to power and influence. Admittedly, the topic of persuasion often brings to mind the tactics of unscrupulous advertisers to induce consumption and the peddlers of entertainment, drugs and sex.

However, persuasion is OK, as long as it is ethical and non-manipulative in a deceitful way. Some people have it, but many more do not. They are the lucky few who possess the natural ability to convince potential employers to give them the job or to persuade their manager that the next promotion should be theirs.

To be a manager you must be an expert at persuading and influencing others to work in a common direction. This is why all excellent managers are also excellent, persuasive salespeople. They do not order people to do things; instead, they persuade them to accept certain responsibilities, with specific deadlines and agreed-upon standards of performance.

Some individuals seem persuasive and act more persuasively than others. What can be especially frustrating, as we watch individuals almost effortlessly charm their way to getting what they want, is the realization that they are no more talented or any more experienced than us. The only apparent difference is that they seem to have mastered the art of persuading others to give them what they want.

Managers hire persuasive people. Job applicants with similar backgrounds, skills and experience, often find it's the most persuasive candidate that is the one hired. As a result, in today's competitive workplace our ability to influence and persuade others has never been so important.

Your persuasion power will earn you the support and respect of your customers, bosses, coworkers, colleagues, and friends. The ability to persuade others to do what you want them to do can make you one of the most important people in your company.

The good news is persuasion can be learned and communication skills researchers have discovered means and methods for improving your powers of persuasion and influencing people to your point of view. In the workplace, employing them can improve your chances of finding that great new job, getting the promotion you deserve, closing sales presentations, becoming a more effective networker and generally increasing your influence at work.

Dear Dave,

As a manager, I must often build support for goals and projects from people who do not report to me. This is extremely difficult, but without their support, my ideas and proposals will go nowhere. What can I do to get these people motivated to help me?

R

Dear R,

There are things you can do, but realize timing is crucial and everyone in every business is quite busy these days trying to perform their work and keep their jobs ... well, at least "almost everyone."

Let me first say that what may seem like a great idea or project to you may not even move the needle on someone else's "gauge of engagement." This means they may not see the value of your intentions and we all know that if someone doesn't see value in something, they won't care.

Gaining Support

Before you can attempt to persuade (sell) someone about an idea or solution, you need to know how it meets their needs and wants (wants are often stronger than needs) and why they should have reason to be interested in what you are proposing (payoffs).

A business colleague of mine tells me he is disinterested in the ideas and projects of others when they seem to lack conviction about what they want to accomplish. There is critical need to be courageous if you have an idea that you genuinely believe will add value.

It helps to present your ideas assertively without being an overbearing, self-serving SOB. Treat the people you are trying to convince with respect; listen to their thoughts very carefully and sincerely; and persevere with the benefits of your pitch.

My 3-Legged Stool of Persuasion

I tell my MBA students that there are three critical aspects that must be addressed when trying to persuade someone about something: the other party must believe the concept makes clear sense to them; they must see "personal value" in the proposal; and they should be a part of the proposal – involved even in a small way.

If people do not see the logic of something, and if they don't tune into the world's most powerful radio station – WII-FM (What's In It For Me) – and if they are not a "part" of the concept by being involved, their interest level is less than zero.

Present Persuasively

It's a simple rule, but be clear in your mind what you are aiming to achieve with your ideas or projects and why they are important. And remember, new ideas and new projects mean that "C Word" – CHANGE – so, again, help people see the value and logic of the change (the why) and *how* it will play out.

Also, persuasion requires that you make clear claims, providing appropriate evidence to support each claim, and explaining how personal needs or preferences will be met.

Handle Objections Early and Often

There will be doubts and there will be objections. Uncover them and address them early and proactively, but don't overly dwell on negatives, because your goal is to be positive, persuasive, and solution-minded.

Finally, don't be afraid to ask for commitment — make it as easy as possible for the others to make one. And, make it clear your ideas and proposals are not self-serving initiatives – they are things that will help make the organization and the individuals successful in this volatile business environment we are in.

Dear Dave,

How can I be heard at meetings? I try to speak up when I have a point and I am quickly trampled over by someone else. Sometimes, I will present an idea and it does not get noticed, but, right after this, someone else says almost the very same thing, and they are treated like they just solved the mystery of life. What can I do?

Stifled

Dear Stifled,

I feel your pain. Meetings often become a free-for-all of the most assertive people dominating the discussion – and discussion may be a kind word. This leaves the meeker getting squashed like a June bug. One public school teacher told me meeting leaders may play favorites (an in-group), who get the most attention.

A little bit of confidence and thought can go a long way to giving you a voice in meetings. Here are some tips:

Have the courage to jump in, but plan your statements — If you have an idea or an opinion, speak up. Start out with a statement that captures people's attention. Identify known talkers in advance and plan ways of handling them.

Be respectful, but assertive — People will listen if you speak in a clear, confident, and calm way. You can say, "Please let me ask a question," or "I have an idea and I want to know what you think."

Give opinions credibility - Provide objective facts such as, "Our experience has shown that..." or "My research indicates that..."

Quit when you've made your point — If you find you are repeating yourself, stop cold. You can offer to write out your ideas in more detail and send them on to the group later.

Ask the meeting leader to establish ground rules - Simple, understood rules of meeting conduct work wonders.

Be a respectful listener and acknowledge the contributions of the loudest members - Show respect and you should receive respect. Also, draw out quieter people for their input and ideas.

Dear Dave,

At work last week, our manager and someone from human resources called us into a meeting room and said the company decided to change a vacation policy, which we all really counted on. The new policy would make it difficult to schedule our vacations. I know it is not always appropriate to say what is on your mind when you are at work, but I went ahead and said this policy was unfair and I don't like it. They said there is nothing they can do and this is the way it is. Later in the day, I was called into my manager's office and the human resources person and my manager reprimanded me for speaking out and even gave me a warning that is going in my file. I thought when you notice something that is unjust, you are able to say so. Now, I feel like my job is on thin ice. What do you think? Was I wrong?

K

Dear K,

I think you have a right to feel as you do, but I also believe it is prudent to handle these types of things in a responsible way that allows you to present your case without angering management. I suspect your manager was embarrassed and cornered, and more so since he was with another person he probably did not know that well.

Every voice has the right to be heard – especially when we don't agree with something. And no opinion can be proven right or wrong – it is just an opinion. The trick is presenting it at the right time, the right way, and at the right place. Blurting out, "I don't like it" or "That's a stupid idea" is going to go over as well as throwing a skunk in the boss' office...which does sound kind of cool, but I digress.

Find a Platform

Becoming an advocate for a group that feels as you do is a great way to voice your opinion. Voicing your opinion in an organized rational way will be the most persuasive. No doubt management knew full well how this policy change would be received and I am sure they were waiting to see who would be the most vocal and how these vocal people handled their opinions. And you, my dear friend, played right into making a messy situation much messier.

Be Respectful.

Your opinion of something or someone doesn't have to be positive, and it doesn't have to be popular. It should however, be constructive, respectful, courteous, and wise—whenever possible—especially when shared with the powers that be.

Being respectful should always be at the top of the list in the way you voice your views.

While I believe this incident isn't the best reason to warn or fire someone, it is legal to fire someone for what you did. In fact, in the absence of race, religion, gender, age, or disability discrimination, an employer can fire an employee without a contract for just about any reason they want, including the situation that you described. It isn't fair, but it is legal.

Obviously, the issue is quite important to you and may others, and the best chance you have of getting anywhere with your beliefs requires a prepared argument in an established meeting using facts as support. Diplomacy and tact are your best tools, not threatening, emotional outbursts.

I suggest you and all employees should avoid losing your temper or simply asserting you are right and the boss is wrong. Politely and respectfully express yourself, explaining your point of view and then step back and listen to the response. Also, avoid emotional language and never directly challenge your manager – especially in front of other employees.

Generally, managers are decent people under pressure to get a job done. Your boss didn't create this new policy, he is just delivering the news. If you have positive criticism which will help them achieve their aims, they will listen. It is in their interest to do so.

In Summary

Remember, even though your manager is higher than you on the totem pole, he is a human being with sensitivities and needs. The best way to have constructive dialogue is to respect him and what he has to say until your point of view can be given and heard.

Dear Dave

I propose ideas to my manager and coworkers that will save time and energy, and even money, but I get looks like I

should mind my own business. One time I gave my manager an idea and he told me, "We kind of like the way we are doing things now." Maybe my ideas are not good. I think people just don't want to try new things. What do you think?

P

Dear P,

Maybe it is the way you are presenting your ideas. You may have valuable ideas, but people may have a hard time wrapping their brain around them. Possibly, your ideas may require that ugly and feared word…change.

Communications theorist, Hoveland, says every communication has three key elements: the sender, the receiver, and the message itself:

The sender is assessed by the receiver for their credibility, expertise, and whether or not the receiver even likes the person.

The receiver may be in either a receptive or closed-minded state, a bad mood, busy, or anxious and this affects their ability to be objective and whether or not they will even listen at all.

Finally, the message itself is analyzed for quality, thoughtfulness, or whether or not it is even something the receiver cares to hear.

Thus, you have these three dynamics going on and thoughts, perceptions, current conditions, timing, and emotions are thrown on top of this somewhat chaotic blend making it difficult for people to communicate. I had a manager once tell me, "Today, all I want to hear is good news. Don't come to me with anything wrong." In essence, he told me, don't bother him with reality and the truth. Denial is not a river in Egypt.

One of my colleagues tells me that no message will be fully grasped by any one if it comes from a person who seems unsure, lacks sincerity, and is about as inspiring as a colonoscopy.

There Are Methods

Dale Carnegie, Brian Tracy, Zig Ziglar and other masters of persuasion and influence believe the magic of communication and human connection is achieved through learnable and implementable concepts and practices. They all believe building rapport, showing deep human interest and respect, and fully listening to people will win them over. Also, the kindness and attention you show to someone who is speaking will be returned to you.

In that vein, people always hate it when someone walks up to them and tells them overbearingly, "Hey, this is what you gotta do!" For many, this feels like an uneducated order, an intrusion, and a violation of sorts. It is best to lead with questions and try to get on a level playing field with the other person so real dialogue can take place.

Involve People in Your Idea

When I was in sales, I always asked for the customer's ideas, opinions, and experiences. Once they became a part of the process, ownership and buy-in followed. I would say, "I have been thinking about something that may help you sell more and make more money, but I need your thoughts..."

Create a human connection before trying to sell them on something. People are fragile and impressionable. They are also proud and do not want to be told something that may show they are wrong. Sadly, many great ideas are trashed, because the people hearing about them are uncomfortable about the way they are presented, they are challenged to give up something they depend on and trust, and because they don't believe they are part of the solution.

I realize I am throwing many potential judgment calls at you, and I am not saying you are being harsh, uncaring, aloof, or insensitive when presenting your ideas. I am only stating that it is important to consider the things that may be going on beyond the potential value of the ideas you wish to present.

If you take time to truly listen to others and deeply probe for their views, ideas, and beliefs, and to build a connection by showing respect. Also, if you bring people into the fold by having them contribute to and build on an idea or concept, they will reciprocate with a willingness to fully examine what you have to say and there is a greater likelihood an idea will get legs.

Dear Dave,

My salespeople often never know when to quit selling and let the customer come to a decision. I also notice this happening with other managers in meetings and with other people at our company when they present ideas. What are your views on not knowing when to quit talking once you have made your point?

T

Dear T,

You are describing the deadly sin of "over-selling." And I'm not talking about selling too much of something to a customer, nor even making excessive claims about a product, service, or idea. I'm talking about not knowing when to quit talking once you have made your pitch.

Over-selling makes buyers start to question their belief in what you are selling whether it is a product, a concept, or an idea. They think you are trying too hard and there must be something else going on that they do not know about.

Often, over-selling just makes people mad. They have heard enough and they will not or cannot decide at that moment, so more information being thrown at them wastes their time, makes them feel like the seller has no respect in their judgment, and may bring any further discussion to a grinding halt.

When to Close

One long-time sales representative and sales manager I know puts it quite simply: "Sometimes you need to shut up and ask for the order. Closing on the sale prevents over-selling. It can be a huge mistake if a salesperson continues their sales pitch after the customer has already decided to purchase."

I believe people are always selling. To get things done, you often have to change peoples' minds and use convincing, reasoned thought to do it. Therefore, the science requires you to know the person(s) you are communicating with, have a logical argument (pitch) planned out, back-up your claims with evidence and support, and then ask for their commitment.

The art is reading people for their readiness to listen, their acceptance of your thoughts, and knowing when you have been successful, or it just, plain is not going to work at that particular point in time and your spiel is going nowhere.

In my selling days, I scored a lot of points and sales with customers, when I realized my presentation was going absolutely nowhere, and I closed my pitch book and said, "This may not be the best time for you to hear all this. Is there a better time to talk? I really want to know what you think and I want to meet with you when the time is right." I often heard customers responding with gratitude that I understood and respected their current needs.

Confirm Expectations

The first step in avoiding overselling is to determine what is most important to your customers or any audience. What are their expectations when buying or buying into your product, service, or proposal? You know what they say about assume. Never operate from the assumption that you know what's best for them and bombard them with nonstop statements that overload their thinking.

We all know that customers/coworkers often give vague answers to questions. This can happen for all kinds of reasons. Some simply don't want to be held accountable or they do not feel comfortable enough to say what's on their mind. Sometimes people are vague because they really don't know what you are talking about and how it relates and adds value to their *real* needs.

Fog Cutters

Great presenters (sellers) excel at cutting through the fog of doubt and uncertainty. They know how to walk people through a learning experience where everything flows, makes sense, connects, and has direct value to them. Presenters are skilled at helping people become clear about their expectations and their needs. To do this, presenters ask open-ended questions (questions that start with what, why, and how) designed to obtain specific facts from listeners to help close a sale.

Then, presenters provide solutions to the listener needs and paint mental pictures in the minds of the listener, so the listeners can actually envision their successfully using the product or working with the proposal to make their life simpler, better, and more efficient.

Finally – and time for the drum roll – presenters clam up, listen intently, ask deeper probing questions, fully answer the questions, and clam up again. It's simply human-centered, needs-driven, open and honest dialogue that ends when it should.

Chapter Twelve: Strategy

Everyone can think, though we often believe the jury is out with some people. Also, everyone can grasp the concept of a strategy and that it entails looking at the situation, interpreting what is going on – really – and planning a ploy to either solve problems or exploit opportunities.

Strategic thinking is the process of developing and evaluating every decision and action in light of current and future circumstances, the direction you want to go in and the results you want to achieve. It involves being able to apply possibility thinking to every situation. It involves the discovery and fulfillment of growth opportunities, as well as contemplating new and better ways to protect yourself from the sneaky competition.

Then, what is strategy? This is the actions and capability exploitation that leads to a significant difference in company performance. The benefits of an effective strategy include: a market relationship of resource and capability; an understanding of the internal/external environment; a framework for integrating activities; and a guide for decision making.

To cut to the chase, a strategy is a "gap filler" getting you from A (where you are) to B (where you want/need to be). It's a blueprint, a systemic ploy, a framework for execution, and a means to measure whether or not you arrived at your B.

Every challenge, every problem, or every action that someone needs to face or embark on in the organization needs to be assessed in light of the broader context. This wider framework will better inform decision-making and ensure the functioning in an organization is done in a more integrated fashion and is aligned to the strategic goals.

Strategic thinking introduces an innovative, new way to think about and approach the troubling business problems and challenges so many leaders are up against today. Strategic management requires the skills, attitudes, traits, and behaviors you need to think critically, find new answers, uncover new opportunities, and make better decisions.

It is important to remember, that strategies are not things that suddenly appear and absolutely show us the way without variance and exception. Strategies are organic – they change and we must constantly be thinking about our thinking, and read the smoke signals telling us to change direction.

In short, while a strategy is being implemented, a company must be observing, monitoring, weighing, and analyzing the environment – internal and external – for changes, factors, forces, and elements that may derail the "current" strategy, or make the current strategy appear to be fruitless nonsense.

Contrary to popular opinion, it is not solely the domain of the top leadership, nor is it the sole responsibility of a strategic planning unit. It is the responsibility of every person working in, or for, the organization. It is also not a once-off activity to be done when a strategic plan is being formulated.

Having a strategic plan is one thing, but having every employee working that plan, being innovative and criteria, measuring and implementing quality, and keeping their "eye on the prize" – the customer—is the ideal. It also doesn't mean blindly putting into action what appears in the plan. It requires time to re-evaluate, challenge, and adjust where necessary.

Just think of the potential if all employees, from first line of customer interface, to clerical administrator, to machine operator, to team leader, to specialist, to executive leadership, applied proactive thinking to their work.

To add to that imagine if every employee and leader considered the environmental context in which they operate, the resources they have at their disposal, the relationships they need to foster, and the most efficient way to operate so as to achieve the best results and sustain them. Can any organization today afford not to enable or encourage such a process!

Thought must be given to what actions the organization can take to proactively influence the circumstances in its favor. Read on to see if my suggestions can do that.

Dear Dave,

The idea of a company vision really humors me. Our company president keeps talking about his vision for the company and we all must work hard to help the company grow and make money. But, all we really see are bad ideas and cost-cutting. A lot of us think we are just trying to make it day to day and we really have no idea where we are going. I'm starting to think vision is making it to the end of the week without closing the doors. I really don't have a question and I am just venting.

R

Dear R,

I feel your pain. It does seem like the concept and purpose of vision is becoming only a fancy word used to tell employees – and shareholders and customers – that the company knows what it wants, intends to do, and where it is going.

However, as we have seen, companies are fighting to survive and any strategic plans may be as long-term as month to month or – at best – quarter to quarter. The economy is so volatile and unpredictable that the government, society, and business environment are all searching for answers and anything that resembles what my wife calls "thinking beyond the end of their nose."

I'm the first one to tell you it is difficult to have and retain a vision when the economic factors and forces are so powerful. But, I will also state that there are often real, long-term solutions right in front of many business leaders, but they choose to take shortcuts and seek only to make investors happy at the end of a month. Helen Keller said, "None are as blind as those who have vision, but cannot see."

Vision is what the company – ideally and ultimately – wants to become. It is that picture of an ideal state and coveted outcomes that *should* inspire the company to not just fill short-sighted gaps, but to do everything in its power to create, innovate, develop, and grow measures and solutions that are desirable, feasible, and viable. In reality, the "brass ring" in the sights of the company is something that is never really grasped, and it is something that the company always and relentlessly shoots for by creating long-term value.

Increasingly, smart organizational leaders are recognizing that some leadership redefinition may be in order. Their leaders may have the *management* core stuff down—setting goals, delegating, providing feedback, running meetings and so on, but there are some critical missing pieces. Many new leaders lack an overall sense of accountability and responsibility to produce significant impact on the business.

Organizational theorist, Peter Senge believes in a rather simplistic equation for producing and sustaining long-term results. His equation works like this: Thinking drives behavior; behavior drives results. So if you want to change the results— and, indeed, change the organization itself—the highest leverage is achieved by changing the thinking of leaders and managers throughout the organization, which will serve as a catalyst for changing the thinking of each and every employee.

Good leaders work on a daily basis to gradually shift attitudes, behaviors, assumptions, and fears toward a desired state. When leaders are involved in and communicate daily change efforts, they set an amazing tone and stance for the whole company. Organizations rely on self-esteem, pride, involvement, and purpose. Leaders that build these critical success factors have an accumulative effect on the "emotional insurance policies" of employees—their well-being, optimism, and inspiration.

Vision is not just articulation of some rosy, possibly unachievable perfect state. It is describing a reality and outcomes that compels people to work hard and stay the path. Employees need more than the "what" the company is trying to become, they need the "why" and the "how."

Employees are gullible, mostly because there are so many "dooms day" theorists and crystal ball experts telling the masses things stink and we are all going to die. Leadership writer, Max DePree, says "Leaders define reality." However, they don't scare the crap out of people and create a culture of defeat and gloom.

Your leadership must describe a vision for the future in vivid terms and articulate values that promote change and adaptability. Employees want leaders who are courageous, are capable of managing complexity and uncertainty, believe in employee capacity and willingness to learn and change, can promote employee accountability and responsibility, and a biggie...learn from mistakes, maintain forward-thinking, and move on.

Dear Dave,

I attended a management conference recently and one presenter asked the audience, "What would you do as a manager if you had one million dollars cash to spend as you want?" The ideas started flying and the presenter wrote them on the board. She then asked the managers to break up into groups of four and create a combined list of what they would do as a group of managers. The lists were very different. As individual managers the ideas seemed self-serving, and were things that applied just to our departments. As groups of managers, the ideas seemed to help the whole company. The presenter said the lists are different because, as groups, there is more pressure to do things that is right for the company and individual managers tend to do things that are most valuable just to them. Do you agree? Sorry for the long question.

R

Dear R,

What a great question, although, this hypothetical situation may be somewhat of a fairy tale these days to have an extra one mil $ to spend. However, I tend to agree with the presenter, but you cannot blame the managers.

Managers try hard to do what is right, but there is great pressure to perform and managers want their departments to shine and, of course, hit the numbers – whatever they are. I think it is only human nature for managers to protect what is immediately important and do what is perceived to be things within their control.

Spending Frenzy — Unfortunately, managers are typically not spending specialists and may not use a strategic framework — such as competitive bidding — to take advantage of available savings. The kid in the candy store mentality kicks in and everything looks tasty. Big eyes takeover prudent brains.

I recall an episode of "The Office" where manager, Michael, was told the branch has over $3,000 left on the books and if they didn't use it, they would lose it. Michael asked the staff for ideas on how to spend the cash and the two most popular ideas were a new copier or new desk chairs. It created quite a struggle between the chair and copier groups until Michael learned he could get a bonus for saving the company cash. Suffice it to say, Michael did not get the bonus and was scorned by the staff for being such a selfish idiot. The moral of the story is: what is best for all is a great idea until self-interest takes over.

The problem is systemic in nature. Managers know they are responsible for specific things and that is good. Hitting

146

goals and objectives is their primary concern. What often happens is managers are not presented the opportunity to see how their part helps to create the whole – the goals of the entire company.

So, managers often work within their restrictive domain and focus only on their defined roles and tasks, and leadership has failed to show these managers how the whole company's desired outcomes are dependent on the function and synergy of what the individual managers do. In essence – stay with me here—the managers may see the machine (the company) as a collection of cogs (department work), rather than seeing how the machine drives and is dependent on the inter-locking aggregate of the pieces.

The Right Things to Do

Spending Triage – If you had the money, I would include positive spending goals like training and education, new resource acquisition, and things that will help your department become more effective and efficient, thus leading to the betterment of the organization as a whole.

Ask employees for suggestions. Talk to other managers about what they are doing or what is on their wish lists. The thing you want to keep in the forefront of your decisions is determining just what will be most valuable to the department in concert with major organizational ambitions and needs.

Immediacy—You want to devote cash to the immediate "gotta have" items versus the dream items. However, I would make sure to dedicate money to celebrating departmental successes and recognizing all of the employees for their hard work. Also, help every employee see how their work and contributions fit into departmental goals, which, in turn, fit into organizational goals.

Dear Dave,

I would love to start my own business, but my husband goes crazy every time I mention the idea and worries about

the risk. I realize that many businesses do fail. What should I know or think about to be an entrepreneur? I believe I have a great idea for a profitable business.

Signed: Sleepless

Dear Sleepless,

Don't do it! Let me rephrase that: Don't do it unless you are ready to commit your time, talents, energy, and often, your financial resources to working your tail off in the hopes of creating success.

When I first went to the local chapter of Service Corps of Retired Executives (SCORE), part of the Small Business Association, to enthusiastically explain my small business concept, the advisory group spent the first 45 minutes telling me I was nuts and to just keep working in the job I had at that time. They were testing my tenacity and determination for starting a business venture. It was a humbling, but very worthwhile thinking experience and tested my motivation and desire

Small business ownership success and survival statistics do not paint a rosy picture. According to the SCORE statistics, 7 out of 10 new businesses survive at least 2 years, and about half survive 5 years.

Small business experts list the following qualities one must be to ensure survival:

1. Self-directed — you must be self-disciplined, self-determined, and self-motivated.

2. Self-nurturing — personal commitment and the ability to replenish your own enthusiasm when no one else will.

3. Action-oriented – the ability to take your dreams to reality with specific, thought-out plans, tasks, and responsibilities.

4. Highly-energetic – emotionally, mentally, and physically able to deal with the punches.

5. Tolerant of uncertainty – not bent on security and comfortable with risks. Of course many of today's workers would testify that uncertainty is present in any position.

"Dave tips" for entrepreneurship success include:

1. Learn from people who are successful.

2. Research your market and idea thoroughly.

3. Set clear and specific, measurable objectives.

4. Network, learn, and ask loads of questions.

5. Don't quit your day job, until your business can support you.

Dear Dave,

We decided to write a new mission statement and discussed the main parts of the mission statement. We all agreed that "integrity" had to be a part of the statement. However, it seems we all have different interpretations of integrity and, further, we are not even sure if we absolutely possess it any more. What is your definition of integrity and how can we be sure we have it?

N

Dear N,

To me, integrity is a concept of consistency of actions, values, methods, measures, principles, expectations, and outcomes. It is brutal honesty in the face of temptation and adherence to moral and ethical principles — soundness of moral character..

Integrity builds trust. However, I believe before you can trust other people, you must trust yourselves. That means you must not be fighting with yourselves in any way, which is fairly difficult during times of great stress.

One of my management colleagues says, integrity is about what you do when nobody else in the world would know or is looking. It is an interesting topic because it is very difficult to determine your own personal level of integrity, let alone a whole company.

Integrity Challenged

We all want to believe we have high integrity, but in reality, we rationalize doing wrong things on a fairly regular basis. We all justify ourselves internally for most of the things we do, or we blame it away on other things and other people.

For example, if we take a pen home from work, it is no big deal, because we frequently do work from home. Then, we drive 5 mph over the speed limit, because not doing so would cause a traffic hazard – and what the heck—everyone else is going 10 mph over the limit.

From an organizational standpoint, there are some times when we do something known by us to be illegal, immoral, or dumb. Or, we deceive ourselves by thinking, "our competition is doing it and if we don't do it, we will get clobbered in the marketplace." This is "organizational stupidity."

Building Integrity

The conundrum is where to draw a moral line in the sand. Here are seven ideas from trustambassador.com that can help the process:

1. **Reward yourselves** – When you are honest with yourselves about something you did that was wrong, that is personal growth, and you should feel great about that.

2. **Intend to change** – Once you have become conscious of how you rationalized yourselves into doing something unethical, vow to change your behavior in that area.

3. **Reinforce others** – Sometimes other people (especially your customers) will let you know something you did, or are about to do, is not right. Thank these people sincerely.

4. **Check In with yourself** – Do a scan of your own behaviors and actions regularly to see how you are doing. Fearless soul-searching is good.

5. **Recognize Rationalization** – We all rationalize every day. Let your collective conscience make you more alert to the temptation to deceive ourselves and others..

6. **Break habits** – Many incorrect things come as a result of bad habits. Expose your own habits and ask yourselves if they are truly healthy for the company as a whole.

7. **Help others** – Help other people see when they have an opportunity to grow in integrity. Do this without blame or condemnation.

Finally, use the "sleep test." If you all can sleep better at night, there is a high likelihood that integrity is alive and well in your organization.

Chapter Thirteen: Teams

I believe Americans – as a whole – struggle with the concept of teams. Maybe our beliefs in autonomy, freedom of choice, independence, and rugged individualism and competition compels us to be more self-reliant and less reliant on the power and purpose of teams.

My students always openly or silently gasp (you can see it in their eyes) when I introduce projects and assignments that are team-based. I know – and they often tell me – they believe that there will be weak links and workers on the team, and that they will need to pick up the slack.

Conversely, some will instantly ponder and plan how they can coast and let the rest of the team do what is needed. There are so many who are skilled at what we term "free-riding," "social loafing," and just plain "slackius superbius" (my term).

We've all experienced problem team members. They just don't fit in with other staff. They constantly snipe at management and colleagues and drop the ball whenever they can. And, they are painfully unproductive, producing shoddy work when they do contribute.

Just as a chain is as strong as its weakest link, so a team is as strong as its weakest member. A single problem member will have a dangerous effect on the strength of the entire team. It only takes one difficult personality on a team to make the team unproductive and the team environment unpleasant for everyone else.

There are ways to deal with these team members and hopefully get them back to being a constructive member of the team.What do you do? Make life so difficult for them they resign or move out? That would be just hiding the problem and these reluctant and incompetent organizational members would just move on to aggravate other constructive and competent teams and team members.

Very few staff try to be dysfunctional team members – though some are quite skilled. Negativity and lack of productivity could stem from a variety of causes; however, if someone is experiencing unusual anguish causing them not to complete team assignments, most of the time, all the rest of the team members want to know is why and then what. Teams thrive on team member communication! Teams – for the most part – do not shoot their wounded.

In conclusion, high performance teams in the workplace can accomplish more together than all the individuals can apart. But, people must do what is expected, work and play well with others, and maintain a positive, constructive attitude throughout the process.

Here are a few team dilemmas and how I respond. Admittedly, I, myself, have failed at maximizing my team contribution effectiveness, but, I think I make sense. You judge.

Dear Dave,

How can we become a more positive team that can really solve the problems we have. What advice do you have that will help me and others become unified and use meetings to solve things and help us end up feeling like we worked together?

T

Dear T,

I am reminded of the quote, "If all you have is a hammer, then everything looks like a nail." Accordingly, we pounce on problems, or only symptoms of problems, without actually defining the situation, coming to agreement on *what is really is,* and how we can use the very best of who we are and what we do to rally our efforts collectively to get things done.

One thing I know about meetings is, you are going to have them. Another thing I know about meetings is, rarely are they done right. Unfortunately, the purpose of the meeting often gets lost amongst the chatter – or spooky silence—and they turn into displays of criticism, subtle finger-pointing, and people wish they were anywhere else than in the meeting.

The term, "Operational Firefighting" applies quite well to the way many organizational meetings are conducted. I had a boss, who felt quite fulfilled, because he "fixed" this or that, shuffled problems around or out of sight, handled everything like an emergency, and never really solved problems. Sadly, this was the way his meetings were run, too. You came to the meeting, he did a quick drive by shooting of personal attacks, and we left the meeting feeling abused and victimized.

How we view things

Many people – when presented some idea or concept – will launch into an endless series of rants about why you are crazy about bringing up the idea and why it will never, ever work. Others (few) will say, "Let's take a look at why this may work." Objectivity – what a concept!

If you want to create and perpetuate what Jim Collins calls the "Doom Loop" in his book, *Good to Great*, it is very easy to spiral into endless negativity, which becomes how you look at everything. I am not saying we should ignore shortcomings and potential problems, but, rather, I believe we should try to create positive momentum by looking for the good in ideas before we dismantle them.

154

Appreciative Inquiry

Have you ever noticed that a typical meeting becomes only an endless passing of information and meeting efficiency replaces the purpose of effectiveness? Rarely is the discussion ever taken to true dialogue where people talk from the heart to the heart. Most meeting work is pro and con conversations about a plethora of issues and, usually, you cannot get people to attend without promising them yummy refreshments.

Problems are seen as obstacles, rather than opportunities to become better and more effective, and keep us from using our thinking, creativity, skills, and talents as innovative growth resources. Also, meeting members are told, "Bring your ideas!" and they are seldom heard nor solicited.

What if we envisioned who we are, what we want, and what we desire to ultimately become? What if we revisit our mission, vision, values, and what really matters to us? What if we clearly laid-out and viewed our assumptions, fears, anxieties, as well as our hopes, dreams, and ultimate outcomes so they can be seen for what they are and not be kept in our mental pockets as silent destroyers of faith and confidence?

Finally, what if we discover and discuss what is right about us and what we are doing, and not just what is wrong? How would this change our ability to truly see and appreciate why we do what we do? How would this lead us to become more of what we are and worry less about what we are not? This is called *Appreciative Inquiry (AI)*.

How it Works

AI is based on the assumption that *organizations change in the way they inquire* and the claim that an organization that inquires only into problems or difficult situations, will keep finding more of the same. But an organization which tries to appreciate what is best in itself will discover more and more of what is good. The good will truly solve the problems.

In Summary

The ability to think is so greatly affected by the attitudes we have. Instead of only discussing what is wrong and where we stink. A positive attitude is contagious, and will provide more effective solutions than a negative one.

Hi Dave:

Based on the way that my department is organized we have started to work in groups and not collectively. How do we create an environment of teamwork and sharing without having meetings turn into an endless checklist of tasks?

Groupie

Dear Groupie:

I discussed your question with a few of my colleagues, who happen to work for a very large local healthcare institution, and they agree with management writers, Prebble and Frederick, who state the purpose of a team is to perform and get results, and the very best managers can gather together a group of individuals and mould them into a team. The writers recommend 10 key differentials to help mold a group into a pro-active and productive team:

- o **Develop Understandings** – Members must understand both personal and team goals are best accomplished with mutual support.
- o **Increase Ownership –** Help members feel a sense of ownership for their jobs and unit, because they are committed to values-based common goals that they helped establish.
- o **Build Creativity and Contribution –** Help members apply their unique talents, knowledge, and creativity to team objectives.

156

- Build Trust – Trust is built when members are encouraged to openly express ideas, opinions, disagreement, and feelings. Questions are welcomed.
- Develop Common Understandings – Members must make an effort to understand each other's point of view. They must listen!
- Nurture Personal Development – Encourage members to continually develop skills and apply what they learn on the job, and perceive they have the support of the team.
- Employ Conflict Resolution – Help members realize conflict is a normal aspect of human interaction, but that situations are an opportunity for new ideas and creativity.
- Use Participative Decision Making – Encourage members to participate in decisions affecting the team. Participation breeds collaboration.
- Develop Clear Leadership – The leader must set agreed high standards of performance and he/she can become respected via active, willing participation.
- Build Commitment – Execution, perseverance, and completion rules! Make sure only those committed to excellence are hired, those that have high levels of hard and soft skill sets.

Chapter Fourteen:
Communication

Without workplace communication, nothing would be accomplished. Instructions could not be given, equipment and supplies could not be ordered, progress could not be measured and services could not be delivered to customers.

The five functions of management – planning, organizing, staffing, leading and controlling – are all dependent on communication. In fact, in surveys of highly successful managers across the nation, the ability to communicate effectively was identified as the most important skill a manager needs for success.

However, studies show that many employees believe their managers are lousy communicators and managers feel the same way about the employees. Why would anything so fundamental, so learnable, and so crucial be something we struggle with so much?

For one thing, there are those supervisors whose verbal instructions sound like something from a Gestapo general and whose memos sound like laws and precepts handed down by a police state dictator. While these messages may be precise and clear, they are not well received by employees. Asking and telling an employee to do something will produce the same result, but asking will not produce the resentment that telling does.

Employees like to be treated with respect and dignity, and, if a supervisor sets the tone and content of communications to do this, it will help develop a more productive and supportive workforce. As I have learned over the years: communicate respect and it will be returned. Short and simple!

We know the organizational "grapevine" is one of the most common – and often the most reliable – form of communication found at work. People talk and they love to talk. When employees know that the supervisor is giving valid information, is not withholding information, and is available to listen, there is no need for employees to go elsewhere to get information. Thus, the grapevine will flourish, but the facts will also be available.

When employees clash, your bottom line suffers. Your office productivity decreases along with morale, while employee stress levels increase along with no-shows. By identifying barriers to effective communication, you can make changes that create a calmer, more welcoming workplace. Cultural, physical, emotional and personality barriers might be some factors impacting office communication.

Listening is just as important as speaking, when it comes to communication. The supervisor who is a good listener is more likely to have employees who help identify and solve work-related problems. The reason is not surprising. Just as we like to have our boss hear and respect our ideas, our employees want us to hear and respect their ideas

Dear Dave,

We tried something in our department that I was not in favor of: Employees were given the opportunity to provide anonymous feedback about their managers and more or less criticize any shortcomings of their managers. It really was not an opportunity to explain what the managers do right, but rather, to detail what we don't do well. I was quite shocked and disappointed by what was said about me. I know there are a lot of bad managers, but I thought I was different and was viewed by my people as someone they could count on. The biggest problem they saw was their inability to approach

me and give me information, or discuss problems. I am trying to stay constructive, so what do I need to do to change these perceptions and ensure I am approachable and open?

J

Dear J,

There is much you can do. First, let me say that the opportunity for employees to anonymously provide feedback about their manager can be a very positive experience, if, in fact, the feedback is not a character or personality assassination and, rather, constructive views that can be turned into changes a manager may choose to make.

It is very important for managers to maintain a positive, productive relationship with their employees, and one of the most important things to strive for is to remain open and approachable. Far too many employers maintain an intimidating air of "do not disturb" that often leads to employee resentment, an intimidating work culture, and problems that could have been nipped in the bud early on.

Don't kill the messenger – Nothing will destroy approachability faster than people feeling victimized – even chastised – for coming forth with information. If you present yourself as a boss who only wants to hear good news, you run the risk of being unapproachable when there is vital – often negative – information you need to hear. Let your staff know that they can come to you with potential problems or suggestions...and mean it. Show them you recognize that since they're the ones closest to the day-to-day work, they may have a better insight into what is really going on.

Open your door and just talk to your people – Simply, being available and inviting is the key to getting employees to open up. You don't need to engage in deeply personal interactions to create an environment where workers feel you take an interest in them beyond the work they do. Sincerely ask them how things are going and what can be improved to help

160

them be more effective. This should be conversational, not hard-core and intimidating.

Study others who appear to be quite approachable — Who seems best at listening to team and individual opinions? Who in the company appears to be "in the know" and has systems or activities in place for hearing employee feedback and suggestions? Look at what they do, even ask for their help.

Other "approachability" tips:

Set aside some time each day to communicate with your employees — You could possibly set up "open for information office hours."

Ask your employees open-ended questions – Ask questions such as, "How can I support you better?" or "What information do you need from me to become more successful at your job?"

Show concern about your employee's personal and professional success and well — being — If you truly care about your employee's success, you will find the time to support them and this will be obvious and welcomed.

Take time to give positive feedback daily – People love positive recognition. The more positive feedback you give, and the more frequent the feedback, the more motivated your employees will feel.

Check your nonverbal communication – Assess your nonverbal actions. Always being in a rush, scowling when people talk to you, or sitting in your office with the door closed, sends out signals that you do not want to communicate with your staff.

When employees perceive a manager as unavailable or unapproachable, they tend to cover up problems. It takes the unapproachable manager longer to find out what their problems are. Also, remember, if your customers and suppliers find you extremely approachable, you will learn valuable things that can enhance or even save your business.

Dear Dave,

My colleague and I were discussing the importance of communication skills for managers. I said that in this day and age, writing skills are much more important than oral skills, because of all of the technology used to communicate, such as social media, e-mail, etc. He said oral skills were more important, because managers still need to talk to people and writing something is not as powerful as speaking it. I said I would write you and get your view, so I can win a $10 bet.

D

Dear D,

Oh no, I will not commit myself one way or another, especially since I teach MBA students and preach about the value of learning and using both superb verbal and written skills, not to forget becoming an expert in nonverbal communication, too.

Survey Says

A study of 35 executives from Fortune 500 companies revealed that most of the executives (66%) felt that a formal course in business communication was essential for success in management, but that oral communication skills were slightly more important than written, because they were used more frequently in management.

Another study of 101 business graduates in lower-level management positions employed by large corporations found that oral communication skills were used more frequently than written at the beginning corporate levels, but superb writing skills were considered slightly more important, because sloppy, poorly written documents, emails, notes, letters, and reports showed the writer had somewhat of a careless disregard for quality and detail, as well as disrespect for the reader.

162

There you have it! Locate different studies and you will discover different findings. However, I am firmly convinced college and company communication skills training should place emphasis upon both oral and written skill development, because you may have the greatest ideas in the world, but if you cannot communicate them persuasively, nothing is sold.

Communication Skills Triage

In written communication, particular importance should be given to informational reports, memorandums, and letters (especially in sales). In verbal communication, importance should be given to presentations, meeting dialogue, interviewing, reviewing employees, and leadership communications (especially during change challenges). Oh...did I mention listening skills?

I recall one study that showed managers found their new business degreed hires were much more competent in writing and listening, than they were in speaking. However, we all know people who can speak well, but speak too much. Sometimes, the best communication is achieved by not writing or saying anything...just employing deep, empathic listening skills.

If you ask any business person or business teacher – or any teacher, for that matter – they will probably tell you that verbal skills have the edge, especially those business people and instructors who tend to think in the "present." The rationale given is people need to "think on their feet" and react and respond in a New York minute to people in conversations, small groups, meetings, presentations, sales pitches, and other close encounters.

Have you ever met a person who can write superbly, but struggles with speech? These folks can move mountains with their written phrases and make hardened souls weep. Conversely, there are so many who could sell ice to an Eskimo (nothing against Eskimos), but if they had to write a letter clearly and cogently, they would fail miserably.

As a teacher, I believe people should capitalize on their strengths and try to remediate their weaknesses. If you speak well and write poorly, work on both, and vice versa. As I do more writing in my ripe old age, I am in awe of those who have mastered writing and have done so early in their lives. However, I doubt any politician would get elected simply because, "Jeepers, that woman sure knows how to pound out and post a great speech on her website!"

So...?

Alright, I realize I have danced all over the place and did not give you the answer you wanted, nor did I give a definitive answer at all. The teacher in me always wanders into rants and diatribes about this and that missing in education and in competencies, so, once again, the soap box was pulled out.

Suffice it to say, you and your colleague should take your $10 and give it to charity. And then, do an assessment of your own verbal, written, nonverbal, and listening abilities, and see what you can do about becoming more effective. If you manage people, do the same and help those folks become better at articulating what they dream, believe, and prescribe

Dear Dave:

My company is cutting costs and is limiting travel to a great extent. The company believes there are ways to work smarter and employees can do more meetings and presentations by Internet or teleconference. Maybe I am old school, but is there a chance that spending less time face-to-face with people going to hurt you in the long-term? I know I get so much more accomplished when I sit down at a table with people than I do by phone or e-mail. What is your opinion?

Signed: I.N. Person

Dear I.N.:

If you are old school, I may have been a classmate of yours. I use electronic communications like most these days, but I also believe that not being in front of people will eventually break down solid relationships, or diminish the quality of optimal discussion and dialogue. There is a lot to be said for a sold handshake and the warmth of a smile.

We live in a marvelous age where electronic communications is getting better and better. Video conferencing is huge as is telecommuting. People are linking up at any time of the day and are reducing the costs and time associated with travel.

I think the answer is to create a balance of electronic communications and face-to-face visits. You need to determine how you can add electronic communications to your normal communication practices without losing effectiveness or deteriorating relationships.

Research what some outstanding companies are doing to balance live meetings with electronic communications. Ask your customers, suppliers, and employees what they would like to see. But, don't forget, people are people and like human contact. If you were to err on the use of either too much electronic or face-to-face meetings, I would choose the latter.

Dear Dave,

At my company everyone is nervous about their jobs and this causes people to share very little with each other. I think they believe that sharing knowledge and information will make them weaker because others will become stronger. Even small tasks get messed up, because basic communication did not take place. Please share your thoughts.

P

Dear P,

You hit it on the head: your fellow employees view knowledge as power and giving it away decreases their power. This information hoarding is unproductive and dangerous.

Most management experts would say that knowledge sharing makes the company tick. Many mistakes and errors can be avoided if folks are "in the know" about things that others may know. Knowledge hoarding also decreases your organization's ability to improve its capabilities and competencies making it less competitive.

Unfortunately, people sometimes attempt to amass power by keeping information to themselves. In every-day business, however, the opposite approach is the most effective. Sharing information is a source of power — the power to successfully complete work demands.

Learning Organizations

Your company must become a Learning Organization. Management theorist, Peter Senge defines the Learning Organization as the organization "in which you cannot *not* learn because learning is so insinuated into the fabric of life."

Also, he defines Learning Organization as "a group of people continually enhancing their capacity to create what they want to create." This requires sharing information versus the way too common practice of "hoarding information."

I would define the Learning Organization as an organization with an ingrained philosophy for anticipating, reacting, and responding to change, complexity and uncertainty. This means people need to talk to each other, learn from and teach each other, and just routinely tell others what they should know.

Power From Sharing Knowledge

The old, paradigm is protecting and certainly not sharing information. As you put it, people are stuck in the mindset that knowledge is power and they only share what they know when forced.

The new paradigm is that those within the organization who unselfishly teach, share information, and proactively look for new and better ways to enhance the knowledge base of others are the ones who will rise within the organization.

This is a shift in thinking and will cause many to panic and resist. As one of my colleagues explains, the only people who fail to share helpful, valuable information and especially innovative ideas are the ones who feel they will never be able to come up with new ones.

Management is Responsible

Management theorists argue that the leader's role in the Learning Organization is that of a designer, teacher, and steward who can build shared vision and challenge prevailing mental models. He/she is responsible for building organizations where people are continually expanding their capabilities to shape their future—that is, leaders are responsible for learning.

Good management practices encourage, recognize, and reward: openness, knowledge sharing, creativity, discussion, and information passage. The saying, "companies depend on communication" is not just a mission statement credo – it must be lived and reinforced.

Good communication is critical if you want the people in your company to all pull in the same direction—toward success. Sharing information isn't enough. Managers should ensure that each and every employee provides others with the information that they need (not too little, not too much) when they need it.

Dear Dave:

Why is it all I see is bad news? The newspapers are full of depressing business failures or bad decisions. We know

the economy is bad, but at my company, everything sent to us has warnings or negative messages. If we need to be confident, why don't companies and newspapers publish business successes or positive news?

Signed: News Annoyed

Dear Annoyed:

I agree that often news stories or company newsletters/messages contain negative content and are often "silent killers" that can turn people off. Many people have set up defense mechanisms thinking the news is going to be negative, so why read it?

However, in defense of some newspapers I often see local and national stories about companies doing good things for employees and the community, or articles about good management and leadership practices.

For companies, the key is to publish what you should and to not publish bogus, unnecessary garbage that scares the pejeepers out of folks. Many companies I have worked for often published mind-numbing, scary announcements on a daily basis.

The internet has even worsened the negative organizational correspondence clutter situation, because now, anybody at any time can blast off a barrage of rants and diatribes, mindless chatter, or cartoons about management stupidity. It is pretty hard to get pumped about your company when you receive an e-mail showing your boss dressed in Taliban attire.

Company newsletters should be lively, informative, factual, interesting, and fun. There should not be content about mismanagement, sales declines, poor performance, or angry customers. The company literature and Internet messages should not be the mediums that chastise employees.

The world is complicated and disappointing enough, so people don't need to receive daily rations of mind-numbing news. They must hear and see the truth, but it must only be a part of a comprehensive communication plan that also educates, informs, and enlightens in simplistic ways. People are people, after all.

Dear Dave,

Why do many people communicate so poorly these days? It's not just when they write, but half the time I can't understand what people are saying. Maybe it's me, but are people learning how to communicate in schools or at their work? Will it get worse?

Kathy

Dear Kathy,

You came to the right person. The preponderance of poor communications skills is systemic in nature considering poor high school graduation rates. The U.S. Census Bureau reported the 2007 Minnesota public high school graduation rate was only 59% and the Minnesota Department of Education showing the Rochester Public School District faring better at 87%, but trending downward.

Minnesota "Garage Logic" talk show celebrity, Joe Soucheray, heard locally on KROC-AM 1340, says it seems nobody finishes their sentence with "ing" anymore. All he hears is huntin, fishin, and askin – or even worse, axin. Like, are you axin me a question? Unfortunately, when bad habits – such as improper language—are repeated by enough people, long enough, they become mainstream and commonplace.

So, what should we be "learnin?" Sorry, bad joke. Communication books generally break business communication skills into three subsets: organizational, leadership, and interpersonal communication skills.

169

Organizational communication skills – these include: making convincing presentations, using information technology, writing business correspondence, initiating open discussion, negotiating, and resolving conflict.

Leadership communication skills – including: arousing enthusiasm, being a change catalyst, building team bonds, providing motivation, persuasion, and building optimism.

Interpersonal communication skills – the one-on-one skills including: active listening, building rapport, emotional self-control, building trust, and relating to people of diverse backgrounds

The question becomes: How can people learn and use these various skills? One word: Education. Colleges, high schools, community education, books (yup, reading more), trainers, and businesses may be of great help. The resources are out there – people must locate and learn from them. There's that personal accountability thing again.

Can we blame *misuse* of electronic communications (e-mail, Twitter, Facebook, etc.) for causing the well-written word to become a confluence of abbreviations, poor grammar, incomplete sentences, and fragmented thoughts (work with me, I am venting here)? The answer is, yes. Can we blame sloppy, incoherent conversation and dialogue on bad habits, laziness, and incomplete education? Again, yes. I won't even get into song lyrics.

Other teachers tell me many students lack basic communication skills and it is very difficult to teach a specific course that assumes students have basic communication skills, and they do not.

Will it get worse? Yes, if we don't break the chain of communication decline. I believe education, business, and – yes, families – need to focus more attention on communication skills. Individuals must assess their communication skill competency and responsibly make attempts to improve. What

170

good is knowledge and having viewpoints if you cannot communicate effectively?

Dear Dave,

How should I communicate bad news? As a fairly new manager, I have been given the task nobody wants: Telling people about company problems and how we are going to do things such as layoffs, cost-cutting, and even taking away benefits. Maybe there is no good way to give bad news. Should I just announce the news and then get ready to run before people start asking questions?

Bob

Dear Bob,

No one likes to get bad news, especially when it applies to one's livelihood. There is no doubt--layoffs are difficult to accept. However, there are communication formats that can lessen the pain.

I am not saying you can make something as devastating as layoffs sound like a Sunday church picnic, but treating people with respect and showing great empathy will certainly help. People often look at their work as who they are, even though there is much more to someone's life, such as family, friends, interests, faith, and health.

Using termination as an example, the message needs to be clear and concise. "Beating around the bush" isn't acceptable — neither is a very brief, dramatic statement like "You're fired." I can just imagine a manager discussing some exciting parts of their weekend with an employee and then saying, "Oh, by the way, pack up your crap, you're outa here!"

A manager I know believes most employees have similar expectations about how they want bad news communicated to them. He says, "They want the process to be transparent and the option to be involved in the change process. This is why it's important for managers to communicate business concerns to their employees when they arise. When employees are aware and have had time to digest the situation, they are more apt to understand and accept difficult decisions."

The following process, recommended by organizational psychologist, David G. Javitch, has been called the "bad news sandwich" because it starts positive, delivers the bad news, and ends with a positive. Even as a sandwich, it is *hard to swallow* (typical bad pun by Dave).

Say something positive, like "You've been a valuable member of our team for some time. I want you to know that I appreciate your contribution." This statement can be better accepted if you are certain to show empathy for the employee.

Continue with the bad news. Tell them you have to cut your losses and terminate some people or cut back on certain projects. Pause and wait for your words to "sink in."

State what you'll do to help out those being terminated. Say you have a program to show employees how to develop their resumes, search for new jobs, etc. If you don't intend to do this, then ask them to finish up what they're doing, gather their things, say their goodbyes, and leave the building by a certain time.

Show respect and concern for the employee when openly and honestly delivering news, even when that news is bad.

Chapter Fifteen: Learning

Describing workplaces as "informal" learning environments may be inaccurate. Most companies have at least "some" method of indoctrinating employees into the firm. These methods may not always be written down, nor may managers approach the education of new hires in a systemic way, but, usually, there is some process used so employees can learn what they need to know.

I recall my first days at some companies I worked for and I can tell you that some had their act together to orientate new employees about the company, the history, the policies, and the workplace. However, there were a couple that just showed me my work area and said, "Have at it!" I'm not sure how I made it past the lunch hour.

Thankfully, there were good fellow employees who came to my rescue, befriended me, and started showing me the ropes. These folks became fast friends as well as valuable workmates. I still remember them and think back fondly picturing how they made time for me and kept me calm and productive.

You cannot get a job these days without some form of schooling. Depending on the job, the education you need could be quite expansive. In many companies these days, one needs a graduate degree (MBA and such) to secure mid-level to upper-level management positions.

Also, you get the old, "We need experienced people for this job." Well, I'm here to tell you there are a lot of experienced people walking around and working, who have no clue about what they are doing - experience may be overrated.

My point is, people learn and they learn at work. We come to work with knowledge, but each company is different in what they want and expect you to know. How we get the needed company knowledge is generally up to us, if there is no formal plan in place. Some tell me that the informal measures – such as the grapevine – teach us more that any formal HR education indoctrination. I believe this.

Let's visit a few letters from the past dealing with work learning and knowledge attainment. We'll see if you learn anything.

Dear Dave:

Here is an interesting dilemma my boss and I were just discussing the other day: While in school a student is well connected to thought provoking and new learning opportunities. It is stimulating and keeps you on your toes. How does one maintain that level of learning and excitement once they are out of school?

Su

Dear Su:

First, let me say I am happy that you decided to go to school and earn a degree. Also, you should be proud of yourself for being concerned about continuous learning and staying on top of things.

Management writer, Carter McNamara, says continuous learning is NOT about continually taking courses—it's about developing skills in reflection and inquiry—it's about learning how to learn so that your life's experiences become your own learning lab. The concept of continuous learning has become quite prominent over the past 5 years. Organizations are changing rapidly. Therefore, it's difficult to find any approach

174

to doing anything in organizations that doesn't soon become outdated.

The concept of continuous learning has become important because it places priority on noticing, adapting, and learning from change. Does all this make you excited?

In short, delve into the educational offerings available through community education, local colleges, and the various seminars and workshops offered by the Chamber of Commerce and other professional organizations. Buddy up with your colleagues, spouse, and friends to enroll in classes and seminars – this will add to the experience and will stimulate discussion after the class is completed. Book clubs are a great idea as well as organizing topical discussion groups. Read professional journals and even join some organizations so you can continuously be sent enlightening newsletters, articles, and research papers.

Other sources of knowledge and inspiration – if you are fortunate enough to have this – are the educational opportunities available at your place of work. If you work at Mayo, you are only a couple of mouse clicks away from an abundance of live and internet educational offerings.

So... be creative, explore, and keep your passion for learning.

Dear Dave,

I manage a pretty strong team. All members have unique skills as well as job skills. The problem is, everyone is in a hurry to get promoted and doing everything they can to get to that next level, but they are not taking the time to become more effective in their current roles. I believe they all know that how they perform now is important and affects their growth potential, but it is disappointing that they spend more time getting ready to move on than focusing on their current role. Advice?

M

Dear M,

There is a great deal you can do. First, think about the individuals on your team and how you appear to them. What is your own philosophy and strategy for horizontal development (growth within a role) versus vertical development (growth out of a role and into another or to higher levels of responsibility) for these employees?

The answers to this question will have great impact on how employees see themselves right now and how they see themselves in the future. In short, what are you modeling and encouraging in terms of growth to the next level of employment versus growth within one's current expertise and position?

Opportunity Hoppers

There is nothing wrong with aspiring to higher-level positions, especially if one is building up one's skills and abilities to be effective in these new, challenging roles. The dilemma occurs when folks are only preparing for tomorrow without living and working for today. This is like building a dream home, but neglecting your current living conditions.

You say something that is right on the mark: If people want to be promoted, they must shine and display stellar performance all of the time. At my college we have hundreds of students completing degree programs in the hope this hard work will gain them better positions. This is all great – especially, because I am an educator – but I cringe to think that they are neglecting their current roles to gain a degree.

As with almost everything we must choose and it may not be a case of just building one's abilities (capacity) for tomorrow, or performing admirably today – it is both. People will be best prepared if they do their best today, while preparing for the next level of employment.

When I interview new MBA students I ask them how they ensure they are effective and what they are doing to learn new skills. I also ask them what a new degree (MBA) will do for them. Unfortunately, I often hear them telling me they want a degree to get promoted and not mention the education and what the education will do to transform their lives, their behaviors and attitudes, and their thinking.

Define Reality

It appears you are close to your employees. I would have informal conversations with each and every one of them telling them how much you appreciate their hard work and desire to improve themselves. But, you must also persuade them to believe their growth potential lies in superior performance ... right now.

Accordingly, calmly convince them – like a "good Dutch uncle or aunt" – that building their future is wise and prudent, but they will ultimately be judged by hiring managers on their ability to do their best work no matter what their role was and what challenges they had.

Dave's "Nugget"

Remember, "garbage in-garbage out." When hiring, get the best people you can find, train and educate them extensively, treat them with respect, and provide all of the resources they need. They will work wonders for you making your job much simpler.

Dear Dave,

Recently, there was a management position open at my company. I applied, but my company hired someone from outside the company and I didn't even have a chance! I feel really bummed. What can I do to improve my chances of being promoted?

Signed, Slapped

Dear Slapped,

First, do not be down, get down... to business... improving yourself further. Do not take this hiring as an insult to you and your skills. I am not defending your company, but it appears they may have wanted to get somebody who would bring unique and different perspectives to your organization.

Be positive! Human resources consultant, Frode Heimen, writes it is always your choice to be positive and if you are a positive force, and implement positive energy into your job, co-workers and surroundings, you will stand out favorably.

I tell my management students, "You cannot sail without the SEA (skills, experience, and attitude)." Jump into your SEA and develop the following major areas:

Skills

Develop your skills further in area colleges, seminars, workshops, and continuing education offerings. Studies show business executives look for these 3 core competencies in people they promote:

Leadership — persuasion, motivation, inspiration.

Communication – written, verbal, and nonverbal skills.

Team-Building — ability to bond, engage, and energize groups.

Experience

Try to hone your management skills through the many learning opportunities around you including:

Outside Organizations — volunteer more, manage teams and projects.

Inside Opportunities – join company process and improvement groups, and study teams.

Learning Opportunities (such as the Chamber of Commerce Leadership programs).

Attitude – I've got a list for this one!

178

- Make sure you acknowledge the good work of others.
- Smile as much as you can!
- Make sure to find a positive view on every topic discussed.
- If what you have to say is inappropriately negative, shut up!
- Take 5 minutes in the middle of the day, just to reflect on the day so far, and your attitude.

And do your job with high quality. Be proud and focused.

Dear Dave.

I see you write about good management, but how can we find out if managers are really doing the best job and what should we be looking for? I don't think many of our managers are doing the best job, just enough to get by. We don't have much money at my company right now for training, but what can we do when we find problems? I think morale is low, too.

"S"

Dear "S"

Ooh... I can't write fast enough to answer your question. First, I will say, do not cut yourself short on hiring the best managers, training them intensely, allowing these talented people to work and do their jobs, and retaining the best at all costs, while shedding the nonperformers. But remember, you want to assess behaviors and practices, not personalities, even though you are tempted to do so.

A management colleague of mine believes a strong management team contributes to the success of the organization as a whole. He states the most important goal for management is to achieve synergy of the talents of the team. Getting by in today's world is not good enough and *good* managers define what the organization is attempting to achieve, and provide clearly stated expectations for accountability and ownership of success.

Ask yourself these questions:

Do managers and employees share a vision, mission, and values for organizational success?

Do we have a system to measure/quantify management effectiveness?

Are internal management practices in alignment with achievement of organizational goals?

Do the behavioral skills of managers contribute to a positive synergistic impact on performance?

Are we settling for too little productivity from our management team?

Do: Conduct an organizational management analysis to provide a factual summary of a manager or management group. This should provide:

- o A vision of ideal management outcomes and desired states of effectiveness, and the current state of effectiveness. Filling the gap between the two becomes your development mission.
- o A picture of a company's culture and the alignment of management groups with the company's goals and objectives.

Actions to Take:

Data collection: Conduct interviews, survey managers and employees, conduct focus groups, conduct manager 360 assessments (getting feedback from many organizational members, possibly customers, too), or simply observe managers at work.

Analyze possible trouble spots: These include: poor communication, distrust of management, inability to delegate, low motivation, lack of commitment, stagnation of ideas and status quo, low performance standards, and workplace conflicts

Use the information for: Developing and enhancing training and education, mentoring programs, personal management improvement plans, and succession management. In-house training, mentoring, and performance reviews and coaching are relatively inexpensive. Use the talent you have within to teach and help others.

Teach and measure: Management development, which may include: communication, leadership, adaptability and responsiveness, relationship-building, listening skills, delegating responsibility, problem-solving, facilitating team success, cultivating individual talents, and motivating successfully.

I need to add that you – hopefully – will find many things managers are doing right. Use that information as teaching examples and **make sure to thank those managers** for their good work.

Dear Dave,

I am just starting out as a supervisor. My problem is that I am not getting much help learning how to be a good one. All I hear is that I need to learn as I go and learn through trial and error. I am really uncomfortable with this and I think I will mess up and make my employees screw up.

T

Dear T,

Your management development should be a "planned" effort that enhances your capacity to manage your team and yourself. A critical skill for managers is the ability to manage their own learning and receiving management development training is crucial.

I cannot understand how your bosses would think that you will learn management best by being "thrown into the fire." Yes, experience is a wonderful teacher, but experience by itself is only a piece of the puzzle in helping managers be good at their planning, organizing, and coordinating duties.

People rely on their managers to help them become productive and fulfilled at work. We know that a crucial management skill in this turbulent economy and work environment is the ability to motivate and inspire employees who are really – and justifiably – nervous and fearful about their well-being and the organization's success.

Basic Training

Depending on who you ask or what you read, "experts" may disagree on what skills and practices should be required for basic, entry level management. However, what you typically find in workshops and seminars focused on entry-level management skills training include: decision making, delegating work, planning procedures, problem-solving, and making those often confusing and ineffective gatherings called meetings more effective.

On top of all this, managers must learn other little gems including technology use, communications, staffing, performance reviews, and employee training and development. Also, you must learn setting goals, resolving conflict, building trust, quality, and "lions, tigers, and bears, oh my!"

One management consultant I know claims that management often involves virtually everything necessary to make companies tick that you can or cannot put on paper – in short, whatever needs to be done. The challenge is to do the right things the right way.

Also, I hate the word, "supervisor." All I picture is someone peering down on their anxious employees like a rat eyeing an ear of corn. Super means incomparable and visor means concealment and disguise. Put them together and you have "outstanding masquerade". Hmm... I guess I like the name "leader" or at least "manager" better.

For You

Somehow you must obtain that little magic pill for management skills development called – drum roll, please – education! How you get it will be up to you and exactly what you should be getting in terms of management and leadership education needs careful analysis and planning.

The best management training often happens at work. Many employers struggle, especially when economic times are tough, to continue to provide developmental opportunities such as management training. However, a company can and should provide cost effective, creative, and meaningful management training whenever possible.

I advise you to approach your boss and explain that you want to be a good manager, who can help employees become the best they can be, and this requires management development, even if it is "home grown" and provided cost-effectively within the company. When it gets down to it, all we really have to solve our business management problems is education.

Chapter Sixteen:
Customers

A customer (also known as a client, buyer, or purchaser) is the recipient of a good, service, product, or idea, obtained from a seller, vendor, or supplier for a monetary or other valuable consideration. In short, if they ain't happy, shut off the lights.

You have rude customers, nice customers, easy-to-work-with customers, honest customers, and a wealth of other types. Some are just so darn fun to do business with and some make you want to Google "pipe bomb."

We know so many say, "The customer is always right." They may not be, but I think we need to treat them right. Accordingly, we need to get very close to them, talk to them, listen to them, and find out what they really want ... and do not want.

When I was a sales manager I instructed my sales reps to never lurch into a sales presentation without building some rapport and finding out what the customer is thinking and what they are going through at the time. They are people! And, they want to be treated like people.

This focus on pursuing new customers is certainly prudent and necessary, but, at the same time, it can wind up hurting you. The 80-20 rule kicks in and it always seems that 80% of your business is done with 20% of your customers. Therefore, your focus really should be on the 20% of your clients who currently are your best customers.

Naturally, we need to be communicating with these customers on a regular basis by telephone, mail, email, etc. – oh, and in person – what a concept! These people are the ones who can and should influence sales and marketing decisions.

Nothing will make a loyal customer feel better than soliciting their input and showing them how much you value it. In my mind, you can never do enough for them. Many times, the more you do for them, the more they will recommend you to others.

Let's explore some questions about and you can determine if you "buy" what I am saying.

Dear Dave:

I have a short question. How can I find out and make sure my customers are more than satisfied?

Josh

Dear Josh:

I have a short answer: Ask them! Continuously find out what they want and determine if you are delivering on their expectations. Take every opportunity you can to really Wow your customers. Management writer, Tom Peters recommends you make your customers "Raving Fans" who become fiercely loyal to you, bring you repeat sales, and attract new customers to you by authentic word-of-mouth referrals. Consider the opposite: Your customers may leave you because you are not answering their questions and... somebody else is.

Dear Dave:

I work for a large wholesale company that has many sales people and we are having problems like every company these days. I work a lot with our costs and I know salespeople are cutting unpermitted deals with their

customers. The new salespeople are learning from some of these sales people. I don't know what to do and maybe it is none of my business. What do you suggest?

Signed: Confused

Dear Confused:

I was in sales and sales management for over 28 years. During that time, I think I saw every dirty sales trick in the book. As a young sales rep trying to hit my sales quota I heard one sales manager say, "I don't care how you do it, just do it." I also worked for a company that fired the bottom-producing 10% of the sales force at the end of the year even if they made their quota. Sales management at its finest!

There may be so much pressure put on sales personnel that they believe the only way they can survive is by cutting unpermitted deals. The sales people lose their perspective of what is right, and succumb to the threats. I am obviously not condoning shady sales practices, I am just explaining them. Of course, we cannot forget some people are just greedy. Dja think?

Business people are only human and often make dumb decisions especially when sales numbers must be hit. Ethical business people would probably never choose an illegal path, but vulnerable and nervous business people will crack when the pressure is on.

You do have an obligation to report what you have discovered. If you don't, you may lose your job should somebody discover you have not come forward with known infractions. Arrange a meeting with a manager. If improper practices are perpetuated, they will become the business norm. Also, the customer will come to expect these outside deals and no permitted price will ever be good enough.

Customers believe the salespeople "are" the company and they associate the practices of these people with the company as a whole. Honesty is the best policy. So, do the right thing and help your company.

Dear Dave,

I am finding telling the truth to be more and more difficult. We are starting to say almost anything to keep customers and employees happy. The pressure we are under is causing us to lie and it is getting out of hand. Help!

Signed,

A Manager

Dear Manager,

Always communicate unwavering honesty and integrity. You must be truthful to your employees, customers, and everybody who may have impact on your business. Dishonesty is a sign of weakness and a poor business strategy that ultimately will cause your demise.

If your clients and employees know you'll always be truthful with them and "tell it like it is," they'll never have any reason to doubt you. Your reputation as an excellent provider of truth and honesty takes years to develop—but it can be destroyed in a minute. The truth is often hard, but business failure and a loss of honor and integrity is much harder.

Dear Dave,

My company tells us about the importance of customers and giving them quality products and service, but whenever we meet, all we talk about is reducing costs and being "lean and mean." I know we should save money, but we are really decreasing the level of care and satisfaction we provide our loyal customers. My manager is trying to work with the budget she has, but I am frustrated that I cannot take care of the customers like we used to, and it is apparent they are

noticing it, too. Are all companies doing this? Any advice is welcomed.

T

Dear T,

No, many companies are trying to increase innovation, quality, and customer care, while looking at ways to trim needless costs. The emerging business credo is "do more with less," when, in fact, some companies are doing less with less. My belief is the companies that continue to carve out new and better ways to serve their customers (and employees, for that matter) will prosper and survive this economic mess.

These days, smart companies know they may have excessive costs and they are asking all departments to assess what they are spending, while keeping an eye on what needs to be changed or improved, or if customer satisfaction is slipping.

I was at a meeting recently and we were asked, "What are the three short (2–3 word) statements that come to mind about your company's current performance?" We wrote our responses down and turned them in anonymously to be plotted on the whiteboard. The negative statements outnumbered the positive ones by three to one and, arguably, reflected the impact of the economy on the companies, but also showed a great deal of negativity regarding less than optimal planning, quality, and employee and customer care.

Because I am often criticized by my wife for being too hard on managers and organizations, I will note we also included some very positive things such as, "driven organization," "market resilience," and "price competitive." However, some of the real eye-openers – which also seemed cathartic for many – included: "misplaced priorities," "lack of planning," and – this one is revealing – "human talent waster."

I am sure there are managers that believe the customer will not notice any little changes that may reduce quality products, services, and care and attention, and that the customer fully

188

understands that we have to cut this or that so we can survive. I'm here to tell you, the customer does notice. In short, they are insulted they would receive compromised value and care, and they believe there must be better companies still offering superior quality out there and they must go find them.

Budget Prudence

During tough times, it is not unusual for companies to issue broad mandates that all divisions cut a certain percentage of their budgets. These are reactive measures that look only at reduction, not improvement. The problem is, these mandates offer little guidance about how exactly departments should achieve those cost savings. So the questions are all over the place: should we start using cheaper material? Do we strip-out the bells and whistles that have made us famous? Or, do we take a little something from everything across the board?

It is important to realize that this process shouldn't be only about cost-cutting and it should be about re-featuring, rethinking, and re-understanding what we do, what we believe, how we can be more innovative, and fully realizing the tradeoffs that are most critical in order to take care of the customers (and employees).

The original purpose remains the same: get the job done and not compromise on those critical success factors that made us a place of choice, while, at the same time, lowering costs. The analysis of tradeoffs when cutting costs should be measured against four core questions:

- o • Is this something that needs to continue?
- o • Is this something we can afford to continue?
- o •Is this something that could be done more efficiently?
- o • Is this something that could be delivered better by being more innovative or through re-engineering?

In summary, the magic formula is not just slashing the budget. Rather, it is reducing unsubstantiated or unquestioned, needless expenses, while assessing the impact of reducing those costs. You can't spend the same dollar twice...so spend it wisely.

Chapter Seventeen: Trust

Many management experts agree that trust is perhaps the most important element of a harmonious, synergistic, collaborative, and efficient work environment. Organizations that have trust among employees are usually successful; those that don't frequently are not.

The two major questions become: how can we build trust in the workforce, and how can we avoid losing it?" Well, it all starts at the very top, since trustfulness—and trustworthiness—can exist only if top management sets the example, and then builds that example into every all behaviors and attitudes.

Trust is a tricky thing: You can't create it directly; it emerges when the conditions (open communication, being accountable, being honest) are right, and when the conditions are not right it simply won't happen. The focus must be on creating an environment where trust can grow. It won't happen overnight; it may take months rather than days, but it is definitely worth having.

Building trust in your work relationships means that you can depend on others and they can depend on you to achieve a common purpose. Trust is built through integrity and consistency in your interactions with co-workers.

Trust in the workplace does depend upon history and consistency—for example, if your leader has disappointed you on a number of occasions by providing poor quality information provided, you will be less trusting of the information he or she provides to you in the future. It is the leader's responsibility to build a history of trust in the workplace and it is an intentional and deliberate process that involves sincerity and honesty.

However, trust is something shared, sensed, and developed between employees, amongst teams, and throughout the company, and is not only the domain and responsibility of leadership. All interactions rely on trust – without it, we live in a very uneasy state of skepticism and negativity.

Let's now take a look at trust in the workplace.

Dear Dave,

As a manager company, I have seen a lot of challenges and changes. Lately, we have had to make tough decisions about people and costs. The employees who have remained after some of these staff reduction changes just do not trust the company and it is like they are waiting for their turn to be let go. It is sad, because we were once a vibrant, happy company. How can I get employees to begin to trust the company again?

M

Dear M,

There are things you can do and they all are in that magical domain called "good leadership." However, it is hard to rally the troops when the generals have let them down, so to speak.

One recent study of some 10,000 employees showed almost three out of 10 employees *actively* distrust the senior leaders in their organization. I believe "actively distrust" means the employees are quite vocal about their mistrust, which could be risky.

This is alarming, yet not surprising, given the business messes we have seen of late. The fact is mistrust could have dire consequences on staff retention, employee well-being, and organizational performance.

My MBA students believe that employees who distrust their leaders are more likely to seriously consider leaving their organization, suffer unreasonable work stress, and are more likely to suffer mentally and physically. Where a high level of distrust exists, an intervention must be done to stop the continuing damage.

What Leaders Can Do

Employees ask themselves a lot of questions when sizing up their company and leadership at any given time. The most common questions include: Are company leaders honest? Does leadership care about me? And, can they do their job? This trilogy of honesty, caring, and competence are at the forefront of judging the "leadership climate."

Company leaders can achieve trust by listening to employees, empathizing with them, being true to their word ("walking the talk"), and treating people fairly. Trust goes both ways — one of the easiest ways to cultivate employee trust is to start trusting your employees.

Studies show trust in leadership tends to decline with age. One study shows employees in their twenties are twice as likely to trust their leaders as employees in their fifties. In view of this, it appears the "more seasoned" employees carry excess baggage of mistrust – assumedly from accumulated "bad leadership" experiences.

Dear Dave,

I know everyone is trying to deal with business survival in this tight recession. My fellow employees and I seem to have lost our faith in the company. We have seen so many poor decisions made lately and I think my company has really taken their eye off the ball, and not paying attention to things. I think that if employees are confident and valued, the business will certainly do better. How can managers help employees feel more confident, so we don't think we are on a sinking ship?

L

Dear L

The link between confidence and motivation is pronounced. In short, confidence equals motivation. It is important to point out that employee confidence comes in two forms: 1. Confidence in their own capabilities, skills, and performance and, 2. Confidence in the company's ability to lead, make sense of the environment, plan and implement plans, and define and execute on the mission and vision.

Everything, from marriage to the economy depends on confidence...and competence. If employees and customers believe in a company, they will be advocates of the company. If the employees and customers are compellingly moved by the company leadership, a defined strategy, good decisions, and great treatment, they will then be passionate advocates of the company and spread the word like driven missionaries.

But, like I said, confidence needs that crucial element, competence. Efforts to create confidence will do no good if substance and rationale are lacking. Leadership writer, John Kotter says, "It's not what or who leaders are; it's what they do." People are savvy to messages of false hope and will even become more fearful if false hope is all they hear, and there is no plan to make hope a reality. Accordingly, to be truly compelling, confidence must be supported by the conviction that comes from the belief "We know what we are doing!"

Why Employees Lose Confidence

Insights from a survey conducted by Harris Polls found that half the workers surveyed are unsatisfied with the level of support received from their managers. Mass reductions in workforce and economic stress have pushed many workers to re-assess their jobs...and their companies. Cost-cutting measures have generated sharp declines in morale and commitment. Some have lost confidence in their organization's chances to succeed. Others question the strategy, decisions and vision of their leaders. They have become disillusioned.

Any manager will tell you having less engaged and committed workers is a major concern and could have a long-lasting and detrimental impact on productivity, quality and customer service, as well as an increase in the risk of companies. I won't even wander into the discussion of whether or not workers believe that their executives are honest and ethical.

In order to achieve the highest level of employee engagement, employees need to identify with the mission of their company, see a clear line of sight from their work to the achievement of the company's mission, and feel that their individual contribution is important and valued. While employees don't need guarantees of a company's success, they do need a reason to believe that their company has a future.

A **Word** to Managers

Readiness is the key success factor. If employees believe they are ready to face the demands and challenges of their roles, and if employees believe the organization as a whole is ready to confront the brutal realities of the environment, then confidence will arise. Readiness breeds confidence and confidence breeds positive actions. When people have confidence, they willingly invest their time, effort, and energy.

The good news is that any leader can rapidly encourage confidence by building trust through unbridled communication and information sharing; creating plans and objectives inspired by input from employees; attracting and retaining excellent talent; and sharing success stories with all employees. To gain the confidence of the employees, there must be expressed confidence in the employees.

But this doesn't mean you must create a pep rally with a band, banners, and balloons. The kind of confidence people need doesn't come from emotionally-charged speeches or from patting people on the back and letting saying you have faith in them. It comes from a well-articulated vision, a definition of purpose, and a carefully crafted plan that guides people toward early successes and inspires them to ever higher levels of performance.

Dear Dave,

As a manager, I know when I have trust and I know when I don't. Yet, what is trust and how can I build trust when it doesn't exist? Also, how can I maintain and build upon the trust I currently have, especially when everyone seems to be out for themselves?

S

Dear S,

I hope you trust my answer. Seriously, trust is something wonderful and when it does not exist, it seems like people would be forced to live in a constant state of self-serving motives.

The best way to maintain a trusting work environment is to keep from breaking trust in the first place. The integrity of the leadership of the organization is critical and the truthfulness and transparency of the communication with staff is also a critical factor.

People are afraid of things they don't understand — providing information about the rationale, background, and thought processes behind decisions is another important aspect of maintaining trust. Are you doing this?

Another is organizational success; people are more apt to trust their competence, contribution, and direction when part of a successful team, project, or organization. If a company is struggling and suddenly no one hears or learns anything – called "organizational secrecy" – trust is 86ed.

A colleague of mine, who does management training, tells me trust instills confidence and hope, and a lack of trust is dangerous—unless trust permeates all facets of an organization, productivity will fall, creativity will decrease, and morale will become lower than Bernie Madoff's popularity rating.

What Injures the Trust Relationship?

Being reliable and consistent helps to build trust. Of course, you can be reliably and consistently a self-serving jerk. But, if employees believe their manager will be predictably fair and honest, then, trust will abound.

Ask yourself: am I reliable … and approachable? This is possibly one of the greatest causes of lack of trust in the workplace. The question people have rattling around inside themselves when they decide whether or not to trust you is: "Is your word your honor?"

Trust takes time: when you first start building trust with others, start by making small agreements and keep them. A pattern will emerge and people will develop trust and realize you will not "drop the ball," which everyone hates.

Also, think about what you are agreeing to – have you ever made even a small agreement that you didn't fully intend to keep? If you say you are going to get back to someone by the end of the day, then that is what you do. Communicate at once if you cannot keep an agreement and carefully and full explain why right away.

Finally, try to involve employees more in every-day decisions. In order to build trust or improve it, it is important to explore every employee's idea, ask questions, and involve everyone in the discussion. If your employees feel valued there is a greater likelihood they will trust management.

Yet, even in an organization in which trust is a priority, things happen daily that can injure trust. Your integrity is critical in building and sustaining an environment of high trust — so your actions must reflect your word.

In summary, your faith in your employees is mandatory: employees want to know you believe in them. For someone to trust you they need to know that you approve of them. If you put into practice each of these elements — trust in the workplace will follow. With trust comes performance.

Dear Dave,

I recently attended a management workshop dealing with increasing the effectiveness of a company's workforce. Most of the discussion was based on the fact that employees are usually not empowered enough to maximize their talents and skills to contribute to the success of the company. What are your thoughts on this?

R

Dear R,

Often, employee empowerment is lacking in organizations and I believe empowerment is an indicator of the health of an organization's people strategy. This means when a company has empowered employees, it is likely to be one where people love to contribute to the company's success.

Studies show there is a strong relationship between an empowered workforce and overall performance. Companies who have empowered their employees are more productive, retain more customers, and are more profitable. They are able to withstand competitive demands because of overall employee involvement and commitment.

Power Gap

In today's business climate, power should not be focused on the personal gain, recognition, or advancement of its individual leaders; instead, there should be a collective synergy found among all organizational members, which capitalizes on the skills and abilities employees possess.

However, we know there is – what one of my management colleagues calls—an empowerment gap in many organizations and the employees just do what they are told – that is all they will do. If they are not trusted to make decisions, most likely, their desire to excel in their work will be inhibited. You can't blame them.

Closing the empowerment gap results in a more engaged, productive and aligned workforce and can have a positive impact on everything from the quality of customer service and employee retention to productivity to driving the major goals of the business.

Empowerment Diagnosis

First, closing the workforce empowerment gap requires support and buy-in from the top down. Without executive support, leaders will not embrace empowerment as a management priority. If it isn't a business mandate for leaders, empowerment becomes an empty promise for the employee.

Many traditional managers fail to understand and comprehend how empowerment can impact their bottom line. Many are focused on their own power and authority and concentrate on ways to maintain their personal power base. Power comes from giving up power.

Even organizations as a whole often hold beliefs and views that run counter to empowerment. They are often shortsighted and ignore the fact that collectively, their members are the most critical resource they have to move forward.

In addition, they often claim leadership and empowerment as primary competencies, but fall short in actual attempts to develop a climate conducive to supporting them. Upper management must embrace the idea that the only potential market power and strength they have is maintained by the mutual efforts of their employees.

Success Through Empowerment

It is important for an organization and its top leaders to understand that power needs to flow to lower-level leaders and employees (those closest to the work) whose tasks, projects, and assignments are needed to deal effectively with critical problems.

Full empowerment requires knowing where the empowerment gaps are in your organization – leaders can simply conduct employee and management surveys to benchmark where you are today and identify areas for improvement.

When an organization practices flexible discretion, it generates higher levels of responsibility and a greater sense of obligation among all members, as all individually feel more powerful and in control of events and circumstances that most directly involve them.

Dear Dave,

I am finding telling the truth to be more and more difficult. We are starting to say almost anything to keep customers and employees happy. The pressure we are under is causing us to lie and it is getting out of hand. Help!

Signed,

A Manager

Dear Manager,

Always communicate unwavering honesty and integrity. You must be truthful to your employees, customers, and everybody who may have impact on your business. Dishonesty is a sign of weakness and a poor business strategy that ultimately will cause your demise.

If your clients and employees know you'll always be truthful with them and "tell it like it is," they'll never have any reason to doubt you. Your reputation as an excellent provider of truth and honesty takes years to develop—but it can be destroyed in a minute. The truth is often hard, but business failure and a loss of honor and integrity is much harder.

Chapter Eighteen:
Managers

Management styles vary from individual to individual, by institution, and what industry is involved. We know this. However, what we also know is that good managers have many things in common and it does not matter who they manage, where they manage, or even who they are.

What good managers share are both operational and human in nature. Operationally, managers exhibit skills such as delegating, training, planning, organizing, monitoring, etc. But, most important, they know how to treat people like people. They listen. They learn. They motivate, console, and counsel. And, they know when people are down and need a boost and something to believe in ... such as themselves.

Let's take a look at a few letters dealing with this touchy, oft-neglected, and oft-misunderstood business of management. I was taught in graduate charm school that management and leadership are two different things. I now say, "Non sense!" These days, managers must lead and leaders must manage. Read on.

Dear Dave,

Alright, I have read enough about managers and what they must do to make employees happy and rewarded and all of the other stuff that you and other writers say, but work is work and things just need to get done – end of story. The economy is bad and our competition is trying to kill us. I

think that managers like me should just get workers busy and workers should be happy they have a job. I'm not trying to be a jerk, just a realist!

A Manager

Dear Manager,

From what I can tell, you sound like a hard worker and expect others to work hard, too. That is a good thing and hard work *often* gets things done. Also, I agree with you that workers who have work should be grateful. Finally, in these tough times, any organization realizes what you realize and the fact is survival rests on out-selling, out-servicing, and out-delivering their competition.

Organizations want results and results can mean different things to different people. A simple explanation is that results are produced when an organization is motivated and applies processes and resources to achieve targeted goals. However, results only tell a part of the story and – just like you – employees crave and need respect, appreciation, recognition, and rewards.

I tell my MBA students there are two groups you need to satisfy each and every day—your customers and your employees. Without fulfilled customers, your doors will be closed, and without fulfilled employees, no customer will ever be completely satisfied.

Therefore, management – as I always try to explain and teach in my rants and diatribes – requires more than accountability and pressure, and necessitates those nasty little employee management nuisances like instilling trust, delegating responsibly, empowering people, inspiring them to contribute and feel they are part of a great thing, and helping them become the best they can be.

Trust Dave on this one: if you make your employees satisfied and fulfilled, they will work wonders for you. In short, they will do the required work and also the value-added things that produce customer satisfaction. Show empathy for the customer and employee.

Dave's Success Equation:

Happy Employees + Happy Customers = Happy Profitable Company

Dear Dave,

As a new manager I still have a lot to learn. For example, I have one employee who is generally easy going, but lately he explodes into angry outbursts out of nowhere. I gave him an assignment last week that he did not like and he stormed off—you could hear him all the way down the hall. His coworkers do not want to work with him and I hate to fire him. What can I do?

R

Dear R,

We all know the workplace can be a tinderbox for human emotion. Some employees get stressed and feel there is nothing else they can do except to rant, act up, and generally be a pain in the ... . psychologist, Dr. Sam Fink, comments, "It is alright to feel anger, how you express it is what matters."

However, this employee seems to be severely acting out and – as you mentioned – this is uncommon for him. You do need to provide a healthy and safe environment for your workers, so it is essential that you devise a plan to deal with this situation immediately.

The Angry Employee

There are a number of different anger and conflict situations that managers will face involving different people such as one employee angry with another, one employee angry with a manager, or an employee just, plain angry with everyone and everything.

Often, employees will exert anger when they believe they are either not being treated fairly, they have a great deal of stress in their life, they don't like who they work with, or they may even hate their job. As much as they want to cope and just do their job, they are people, and people are emotional.

A hostile work environment will be created by a disgruntled coworker. In addition, the other employees will watch very closely to see how managers handle angry employees.

For You

When an employee expresses anger, deal with it as soon as possible, and you must show an intense desire to make time to handle and discuss the situation. Many performance problems reach crisis proportions as a result of delay in dealing with anger.

Also, let me add that you should take the time to explain this situation to your immediate boss or HR to document the situation and to explain you are going to handle it calmly, firmly, and effectively.

Call a meeting with him and make it clear to him you intend to find out what is really going on. Your discussion must be private, since it appears your employee does not care who hears what. He may even get a charge out of the fact that people *do* hear him spew his anger, as strange as that sounds.

Try to develop a positive climate and show him respect. It may be that his outbursts come from his not feeling respected. Allow him to talk and don't interrupt. If he is hesitant to talk, show empathy and draw out what he is thinking.

Make it clear that what is happening is affecting other employees, productivity, and the general work culture, and it will not be tolerated no matter what the reasons are. At the end of the discussion, check with him to see how he is feeling and tell him you expect him to report back to you how he will handle his anger.

Allow him to think about the situation, then follow-up in a day or two. Consider the fact he may need professional help or termination.

Chapter Nineteen: Co-Workers

Dictionary definition of coworker: someone with who one works; a companion or workmate. This sounds nice, doesn't it? A coworker works along-side you, is there for you, and is a partner in task completion. Sweet! However, we know that this is not always the case.

Coworkers are not us; they have emotions, wants and needs, motivations, interests, and they often come to work with more "baggage" than the Kardashians going on a 6-week tour of Europe.

In fairness, coworkers are teammates and we should and often do work and play well together, building on each other's strengths, while taking care of tasks and challenges. Coworkers often become close friends and are there for us when we have pains and anguish, and are also there when we just, plain need someone to talk to or vent to.

During the course of your career, you won't see eye to eye with all your coworkers. But you can minimize problems if you apply a few tricks to ease the tension. These tips can help you resolve — or at least survive — those sticky situations.

As I have stated throughout this book, I am not a divine HR know-it-all. In fact, I still struggle to get pumped up to work with certain people; I get somewhat nauseated when I hear total nonsense come from people's lips during meetings; and I continually anguish over the fact that far too many people drop the ball on tasks and expectations – Grrrr!

Let's peek at some coworker situations and you can conjure up what you would do in response. I am only printing what I thought could be thoughts or solutions. Often, I'm pretty good at telling people, "Deal with it. Move on. And, get over it."

Dear Dave:

I have a confession—I can't keep my nose out of other people's business at work and always try to butt in with my ideas and solutions. I am not even a manager and just one of the department employees. I don't know why I have this need to constantly impose myself on people. Last week, one of the other employees finally told me to leave her alone and she will figure it out herself. Is there hope for me?

Too Helpful

Dear TH,

First, let me say, you are probably well-intentioned and feel you have a lot to add, and God bless you. The problem is the way you are going about it and (ahem) shoving your knowledge down people's throats.

Studies reveal most – a majority – want to think on their own and solve their own problems. However, there are many who look at you with those puppy dog eyes and say, "Do something to help me!" One of my business associates tells me you must learn to know when to help and when to stay out.

It is good to share knowledge and companies thrive on employee knowledge. But, first try asking people if they want help. If yes, then help. But remember, people take pride in being a part of the solution.

The most powerful people in organizations are those with no formal authority whatsoever. These are the "go to" experts and everybody knows who they are and believe they can go to these people for help and information. However, these informal experts do not inundate people with what they know... they are just ready, trusted resources.

I believe you should keep on looking for opportunities to help, but you must measure whether or not it is desired.

Dear Dave,

I like my job, but I can't stand the cliques in my office. There is a little group of people, who not only hang out together, but spend most of their time bad-mouthing others in the office who are not in their clique. I am afraid if I do not join this group, I will forever be a target for them and be left out of most everything. Advice?

R

Dear R,

It may be easy for me to say this, but who cares! Groups (cliques) can form around things people have in common, but if you have nothing in common with these folks, "fuhgeddaboudit!"

Much like clubs or gangs, your coworkers are naturally drawn together because they share similar interests, they make each other feel special and a part of something, and they grew up that way and don't know any other way to organize their emotional lives or get what they want.

Some groups - like the one you mention—stick together for a long time. Others drift apart after a while as people move different jobs, make different friends, or just find they really don't like each other and have less in common.

Clique-ology 101

There's safety in numbers. Cliques usually have a strict code of membership and ways of acting and talking to each other. However, instead of being centered on shared values and beliefs, many cliques tend to focus on maintaining their false popularity—most like to think they are "better" than those outside the clique.

I am all for groups of people to bond at work, but, sadly, cliques sometimes use their power to hurt others on purpose, either by excluding them, being mean, or both. Often, these groups take breaks together and have "happy hours" where no one else is invited to join in.

One manager I know says every company has these little factions of employees deciding which employees will be admitted in or excluded from their little circle of trust. Unfortunately, these groups are closed to any perspectives other than their own and may be missing out on opportunities to network and expand their careers.

Often, people like to just follow others and cliques provide that. It's usually clear to clique members what they need to do to fit in. Sometimes that means sacrificing some freedom and following the "leader" – every clique has one.

These leaders are membership control mavens and decide who should be in or excluded. This type of membership control usually happens because the clique thinks they are special and they need to protect that feeling of specialty. They're special alright ...!

Also, using social network sites, these folks have greater power to spread their word at the speed of light. I call this "cliques with clicks." Or, here's another one, "Net Cliques."

Surviving Cliques

How do you cope with these cliques? Know yourself and your values, interests, and beliefs. Ask yourself if you want to be part of a group because you need to feel accepted, or because you actually share their values? Would membership make you feel good or bad?

Remember, cliques can be very limiting in the way they control how members look, think, talk, and behave. True coworkers, who are good people, will respect your mind, your rights, and your independent choices.

And, finally, if you know that a clique is bullying or intimidating you and others, let management know about it and stress that the behaviors and attitudes are hurting productivity and employee well-being.

Dear Dave,

I have a team problem. There are a lot of good people that I work with, but there are also some who never pull their weight and contribute to team success. It's worse than "slacking"—these people do not contribute at all. I know there are tons of advice on team motivation, but can you just please provide me some basic advice?

R

Dear R,

Let's first address the common problem of slacking by defining the behavior. Slacking is when a team member is not performing as per expectations. Actually, slacking is virus (contagious) that can hit your team environment at any time!

My first thought is you should leave the managing to your manager, but if your boss is oblivious to the situation, or just doesn't care, then things should be done to handle the problem. But, be careful, the slacker(s) may be friends or favorites of the boss.

I think before you decide your coworkers are totally worthless, it's best to determine the reason for the poor performance. If an employee's skills are inadequate, this could be a cause of the problem. So identifying the reason for the problem is the first step in addressing it.

Slack-Handling

Usually, your first step will be to meet with your slacker colleague(s) in private. Let them know how their poor performance is impacting your own work and that of the team. However, you do have several other options.

Your next option is to ignore the situation and go about your business. I know it's annoying and unfair that they are getting away with only doing a fraction of the work, but eventually, their poor performance is going to catch up with them.

However, if your colleagues' "slackery" is having a negative impact on your work, or that of your team mates, then you need to take action by picking up the work your colleague isn't doing. This will take care of neglected tasks, but may add to your stress and frustration.

Another, and likely best, option is to get assertive. Strength in numbers is a good way to show them that you mean business — pick a couple of your teammates to meet with them. Be clear but tactful: it's better to approach them in a pleasant but tactful manner, rather than an accusatory one.

Time to Bring in the Boss?

One HR manager I know says that if, in spite of your best efforts, your colleagues won't improve or change, and if their laziness is still causing problems for you or your team, then you might have to speak with your boss. Before you do this, remind your colleagues again that you'll have no choice but to go to your boss if their behavior doesn't change.

In the meantime, make a note of exactly what your co-workers are (or are not) doing. If they spend two hours at lunch and don't make up the time, write this down. If they are making personal calls, or surfing the Internet, write down the times and any other relevant information. Then, hand the situation over to your boss completely. After all, you've now done all you can.

Remember, if you escalate your concern, do it tactfully. It is not taboo to go over the head of a coworker who is playing the system and doing nothing of value. If you decide to talk to your boss, do it considerately and tactfully. Focus on facts, not feelings and put dignity ahead of blame.

Dear Dave,

My company started a mentoring program and I was given a mentor. The problem is, this person is always criticizing things and is very negative about almost everything. I can hardly stand to talk to him, because he brings me down whenever I am with him. I was excited to get a mentor, and now I want to get rid of one. What can I do?

P

Dear P,

Your company means well, even though your mentor does not. Unfortunately – and I have no reason why – you were given someone who was not screened very carefully to determine if they are mentoring material.

First, don't lose your interest and excitement in being mentored. I believe having both informal and formal mentors are constructive and can teach the mentored many things about job performance, the values and culture of the company, and any pitfalls to watch out for.

Also, do not take all this personally. Obviously the mentor has bigger issues and you are just one small part. I do understand how a "negative personality" and a bad attitude can bring down even the most enthused mentoree.

Why We Need Mentors

No matter how much we grow or change, one aspect of our beings remains the same. We all still look to those who have come before us to serve as good examples. As professionals, we seek out mentors whether we know it or not.

A mentor is someone who can help you advance your career, solve problems, think differently, view new possibilities, avoid wasted steps and energies, select new habits to replace old habits, and change to just plain become better people.

Mentors can also open doors for you and introduce you to other people within their network. And they do this for the sheer satisfaction of helping you to grow and succeed.

How Mentoring Relationships Go Wrong

For mentees to benefit, mentors must show an active interest and act in a positive way to advance their career and personal learning. Most mentors have every intention of doing that, yet, they sometimes end up neglecting their mentees.

Mentors may be preoccupied with challenges in their own careers, excessively busy from a heavy workload, or insecure about their standing in the organization causing them to be evasive when called upon for advice or support. Such neglect can lead to mentees' feeling that their mentors don't value the relationship.

For You

Have you spoken to your mentor to let him know how you feel? It is possible your mentor thinks he is doing a good job and may actually be oblivious to the negativity he is spreading. Possibly, if he can see how his negative rants and diatribes are affecting you, he may back off a bit and get to the purpose at hand.

Also, is there a mentor-mentee coordinator you can speak to for guidance? If someone is in charge of these relationships, I am sure they want to know if they are working or not. I would explain that you need someone who can best fit your career desires and the current arrangement may not be optimal.

Finally, you can just bear the brunt of your mentor's negativity and also seek to find "informal mentors" within your company or outside of your place of work who can coach, guide, and help you grow. Mentors are everywhere and most are very willing to help those who aspire to improve.

Dear Dave:

Our office is so full of politics and it is literally making me ill. Everybody is out for themselves and they will stab anybody in the back, if it will help them get ahead. This is not true for everybody in the office, but it is for most. It is getting to the point where I will not trust anybody, because I believe if I tell somebody something, it will somehow be used against me. What should I do?

Signed,

Chris

Dear Chris,

Ah yes, politics is not just in government; it is everywhere. Sadly, there are many who believe that the back-stabbing you mention will help them excel in the organization, when the fact is the people who use politics as a weapon will never be trusted by anyone.

I believe you should take the high road and never lower yourself to such behaviors. I know it is tough when people are causing you misery, but I believe that in the whole scheme of things, ethical behavior will eventually rule. It may take time and the frustration is great, but you will be able to pass what ethics writer, Carol Bly calls the "sleep test," which is being able to sleep at night knowing you were fair and honest.

One manager I know tells me you will never stop organizational politics from happening. It is often practiced most by insecure people with small minds, who are using politics to make up for their inadequacies. Believe me, *good* managers see these games and will not trust these people either.

If the politics are extremely malicious, you have a duty to report the practices and detail how it is hurting both you and the company. Management does not want anything occurring that will ultimately hurt people, productivity, reputation, and profits, and politics most certainly does, especially when it causes good people to leave the organization. Also, politics carry beyond the internal organizational structure and may be sensed by customers and suppliers. They may choose to not do business with companies and individuals they cannot trust.

Rise above all this, my little warrior. Besides, if you leave, you will probably just join a company with a fresh batch of politics for you to deal with. Typically, one or two firings (or suspensions) of political mind-game proponents will put the kybosh on further occurrences.

Dear Dave,

At my company many people are out for themselves and only doing things that will benefit them, and not the company. I am a competitive person, but this is taking it too far. How can we understand what each of us wants should be something that can benefit the company? It's like we are constantly fighting each other for selfish recognition.

Concerned

Dear Concerned,

First, let me say that I believe respectful debate and varying perspectives are mandatory for organizational improvement. However, self-serving behaviors and unhealthy competition are not. Leaders must inspire creativity and organized dissention, while selling unity of purpose.

Carole Nicolaides, of Progressive Leadership, Inc. believes internal competition can destroy your organization. She writes, "Internal competition drives business results" has become a mantra of U.S. companies and has actually backfired reducing communications and causing information hoarding.

I believe that internal competition can become so damaging that it leads to isolation of information, loss of employees, and corporate disloyalty. The solution is to create a

216

true "team" environment improving the "corporate good" through collaboration and sharing.

One business and information technology consultant I know believes organizations need to provide employees what they expect of them in clear and certain terms. He says, "One way of accomplishing this is to require employees to include in their goals and objectives what they will accomplish to help achieve the organizational goals, both individually and collaboratively. This could provide the employee buy-in and accountability. The employees' goals and objective can then be part of periodic evaluation reviews to continue moving in the organization's direction, not just one person's direction."

Unfortunately, the reality is different, people are still getting compensated and evaluated based on factors that kill knowledge sharing and team synergy including:

- o individual contribution (employee of the month)
- o performance evaluations that give only a few people the highest evaluation simply because everyone can't have an "A"
- o forced distributions on merit such as if one employee within a department receives a raise then another cannot
- o contests between employees for various monetary and non-monetary prizes

Quality management guru, Deming, argued that relative performance evaluations and merit ratings breed internal completion, and causes leaders to label people as poor performers, even though their work is well within the range of high quality.

When employees are trying to "look out for only #1," how can we expect to produce knowledge sharing and organizational cooperation? Here are some management tips to overcome unhealthy internal competition:

8. Hire and reward employees based on their ability to work cooperatively to reach corporate goals.

9. Fire people who destroy united communication.

10. Focus people's attention on identifying opportunities rather than competing with one another.

11. Create new compensation measures based on team goals.

12. Promote employees who have a history of building collaborative and unified teams.

The bottom line is that internal competition can create rifts within teams. Companies must sell employees on the benefits of true knowledge sharing and collaboration.

Dear Dave,

So much is said about people with Emotional Intelligence being important at work. Don't they really mean smart people are important and companies should hire the smartest people?

Wondering

Dear Wondering,

Emotional Intelligence (EI) describes the ability to identify, assess, and manage the emotions of self and others. I believe you can be smart and still be emotionally disabled.

EI expert, Daniel Goleman, claims that EI includes four types of abilities:

- o **Self-awareness** — the ability to read one's own emotions and recognize their impact.
- o **Self-management** — involves controlling one's emotions and impulses and adapting to changing circumstances.
- o **Social awareness** — the ability to sense, understand, and react to others' emotions.

o **Relationship management** — the ability to inspire, influence, and develop others while managing conflict.

It all sounds like basic leadership stuff, eh? However, there are many people who can solve the hardest technology problems and not be able to communicate their way out of a paper bag.

Studies show employees with low EI get higher task responsibilities and less "people" responsibilities. Conversely, employees with higher EI tend to be given more people management responsibilities. Of course, we know this is not always true and we all have worked for managers with no people skills whatsoever.

Dear Dave,

I work for a large company. My question is, why can't people complete things? It seems we start things well and we even get excited about some work, but things don't get finished, and there is always one more reason to keep analyzing something, or checking this or that, or we just lose interest.

T

Dear T,

At work people often get very interested in something, take it up with great enthusiasm, and a day, week, or month later it's with all the other things that are on hold.

What happened? I call it "Organizational ADHD." The ability to stay committed and focused gets so easily derailed because we are jumping around like toads from one thing to the next. If everything is a priority, then nothing is.

Excuses

Teams flounder on project completion and then you hear a lot of excuses according to one business person I know. She tells me she often hears people saying things like: We can't pick out the right activities that fit into our time schedule; we just can't overload ourselves with too many things at once; and, it is just so difficult to prioritize our activities.

The reality is, yes, there may be priority, time, and overload problems, but those things are not reasons to prevent things from coming to closure ... at least sometime during our lifetime.

Completion Personalities

First, we have the *"get er done"* Type A maniacs (I'm Type A, so I confess) who can't wait to finish something and they proudly proclaim, "Yay! We got it done!" when whatever was "completed" may be full of gaps, flaws, errors, and every ineffective shortcut known to modern civilization.

We also have what I call the *"Oh my God, we can't finish this, because it is part of me"* people. They have grown so attached to a project, assignment or task that they cannot bear to part with it. The work is comfortable, they know what they are doing every day, they know the people, the routines, and the chores, etc. So, finishing it instills pure panic, because – if they finish the work – they would need to learn new things, work with different people, and generally it would upset their nice, neat orderly flow of what they have come to love and depend on.

Finally, we have the *"I can't make a decision"* people. They absolutely will find every excuse under the sun to form another committee to check on something, or proclaim that we need more data and information, or the thought of committing to something – by making an explicit decision – absolutely scares the pejeepers out of them.

For Managers

Regarding project closure, the manager must define reality and tell people very distinctly, directly, and succinctly that the project is done. One manager I know simply tells her teams "It's over. Deal with it. We must move on."

When a manager encounters delay and completion-avoidance problems, where an employee or team does not execute and complete assignments to expectations and timelines, it may prove valuable to explore several possibilities including:

- o **Criticism** — The employees may fear criticism for not doing things right and completion sets them up for the final report card.
- o **Self-confidence** — The employees may lack self-confidence in some aspect and lack skills and knowledge needed to fully complete the assignment.
- o **Over-dependence** — The employees may be too dependent on the manager and lack the conviction to make those tough final decisions.
- o **Motivation** — The employee may feel like the incentives and recognition for doing a difficult job and bringing it to closure is lacking.
- o **Resources** – It may be that the employees do not have the necessary resources to complete the work and they are not sure how to acquire them.

Often, we find employees who suffer from the above are very nervous or apathetic about bringing things to closure. And, you can't blame them to a large extent — completion is so final and requires closure commitment.

This is when mentoring, coaching, or training kick-in to raise skill levels and confidence. Managers must stress to employees the value of implementing goals, objectives, tasks, and roles, but also coach employees on how to wrap things up. **Oh, and reward employees for successful completion.**

Dear Dave,

Why is it that so many people these days have become good at putting things off and not taking care of business? It's almost like they enjoy the idea of getting things done in the last minute. This drives me nuts, because I pride myself on getting my work done and doing it well. I think when people put things off the work they finally do get around to doing is low quality. My managers seems to be OK with letting people delay things and then rush like crazy to complete things.

N

Dear N,

You are preaching to the choir: I often see procrastination in epidemic proportion. To make things worse, do we take pride in our having developed a "Mañana Attitude" where we believe everything can be put off until tomorrow and things will just "take care of themselves?"

I'm reminded of the quote – I can't remember who said it – "If it wasn't for 'last minutes' nothing around here would ever get done." Procrastination is not indicative of a covet for perfectionism as we sometimes lead ourselves to believe; it is indicative of a "learned helplessness" and "approach-avoidance."

Why We Delay Things

First, let me state that the development of healthy and productive work habits need time, attention, thought, and effort. Sadly, these may be considered laborious ingredients for success and the gentler, simpler route is avoidance and most certainly delaying things.

You are correct when you state that people have actually developed a sense of pride in establishing an ability to take care of things in the last minute. I sometimes see this in my students and I remind them that the quality of the work they do will increase if they attack things early and often. They often look at me and think, "Oh yeah, well you're just old!"

Why do we try to avoid consequences when delay only makes it worse? I think it's part of our human nature, a combination of a desire to avoid pain, and a cocky belief that we can get away with it. So what can we do about it?

Don't avoid the warning signs – things that need doing are really quite apparent to us – we know what they are. When something seems urgent, it probably is. I am not saying we should run around pouncing on everything like it is the end of the world; I am just stating that first things must be done first. I'm reminded of the Nike slogan, "Just do it!"

Doing nothing is a choice too — it can be tempting to think that by doing nothing we are not actually choosing to do nothing, we're just avoiding the situation so we can think about it. But the truth is that doing nothing is as much of a choice as taking action.

Learn from your mistakes – we need to reflect on and think about what negative – even devastating — things have happened because we have not addressed challenges promptly. Ben Franklin said, "A stitch in time saves nine." Not only will we increase the quality of the work we do, if we just plain get busy, but we will sleep better at night from being less stressed out.

In summary, I know we all lead busy lives – and we choose to do so for the most part – but we set a good example for others (especially our children) if we just take care of things, and take care of them effectively.

Dear Dave,

Personally, I expect a lot out of myself and I used to expect a lot out of other people. In other words, I hold myself to a very high standard and I used to hold others to that same very high standard. When I say I'm going do something, I do

it. **Holding other people to a high standard has resulted in lots of feelings of disappointment.**

S

Dear S,

I know exactly what you are saying. Nothing is worse than relying on someone to come through with something just to get slapped in the face by their failure to do so.

Even worse is when you have to chase these people around just to find out whether or not they lived up to your agreed-upon expectations. The response you will hear 9 times out of 10 is, "Yea, well, I just didn't have the time." Then tell me that ... so I know not to depend on you!

Coping with the "Ball Drop"

I'm big on not looking at surface issues, and trying to find the root cause. So, I try to analyze the situation and if they keep coming up with off the wall reasons for dropping the ball, such as, "I couldn't finish the report because my cat hid my car keys."

Over the past couple of years I've been able to conquer those feelings of disappointment very simply—I stopped holding others to "my" high standards. It's not my place to hold others to a high standard, if I am not their manager or father. They must make that choice.

My wife always tells me to quit trying to find perfection in an imperfect world. I understand this, but when your work depends on the functions of others, a whole lot of stuff never gets done, or gets done so poorly it's barely recognizable let alone acceptable.

Don't get me started on how we have progressed – or regressed – to the point where everything is considered "excellent" or "awesome" or "outstanding" when these things are probably mediocre at best. I still believe that excellence must be excellent.

224

I'll See it When I Believe It

If you have people in your life who constantly go back on their words, it will become so normal to you that it will begin to creep into your own personality. The tough part is when people are inconsistent with their delivery and you never know what they will produce and when … if at all.

We know the people we can never rely on for both timely delivery and quality of a piece of work. We can say, "Well, Bob is doing this piece or that and we'll get it late and of low quality." We are somehow OK with that, because we have low expectations of ol' Bob – he's incompetent.

How Do You Avoid Disappointment?

First, don't allow your happiness/fulfillment to come from outside forces that you have no control over. If you can't control a situation, or certain people, you're setting yourself up for disappointment.

Second, associate with people who deliver and deliver quality work – those awesome people that hold themselves to a high standard and won't disappoint.

Third, when you are forced to depend on those who you know will do little, or lousy work – and will even be late with this crap – know it, expect it, and don't set yourself up for the disappointment. Also, know you will probably end up doing or redoing the work anyway.

Chapter Twenty: More Management Stuff

Management Guru, Peter F. Drucker, says, "So much of what we call management consists in making it difficult for people to work." What I read from that statement is that – often – managers just get in the way and should let good, skilled people do their work.

This also means that managers should give it a rest and not feel compelled to always need to be checking this or that and over-analyzing everything about everyone. If you hired good people and if they are skilled, motivated, and know what to do … encourage them, but to not smother them with – God, I hate this term, "micro-managing."

What I want you to take away from my rants, here, is that even good managers muck things up. New managers who have not yet "cut their teeth" on good management practices, nor have they developed an effective management style, tend to be over-excited about their new positions and – even though they mean well – all they do is bother people.

To be fair, good managers often get, inherit, or hire bad employees – it's a fact of work life. I feel bad for these well-intentioned managers, because they want to produce and certainly want to motivate and get to know their employees by developing rapport and relationships; what they sometimes get are people who try to do as little as possible, poison the workplace with their negative, destructive personalities, and may even incur more severe infractions such as theft, sexual harassment, or inflicting bodily hard upon others.

I feel for managers – especially, mid-level managers – they/you have a tough, tough job. Let's read some letters from managers who have problems and struggle for answers. I try to help – I really do – but, sometimes, they need to just get busy, or get tough, or start over with certain people and situations. Like I tell my MBA students, there is a big difference between nurture and coddle.

Dear Dave,

I have tried everything to win over my employees, but I can tell there is a wall between us. What can I do to get closer to them? It would be easy to just be a cold boss and not worry about it, but I care for these people.

R

Dear R,

The fact is there are more questions than answers to this common management dilemma. Managers have a tough job. As long as managers must manage, and as long as employees must produce, there is always going to be some tension between them.

Some managers have found ways to get close to their employees – as one manager tells me, the challenge is to not get so close that nothing gets done. He calls this "country club" management. However, driving a wedge between employees and management creates mistrust, discomfort, and even a "me versus them" culture.

I believe the solution to manager-employee relationships is not either a "beat on them" or "love them unconditionally" arrangement; it is a matter of building bonds and creating a culture of trust and support, meshed with good old-fashioned management practices. Dare I say the "holy grail" is a matter of blending management with leadership?

What Employees Want and Hate

When you were an employee: what did you crave in the work environment? What did you hate and criticize? And, what things seemed to be going well? Amongst your answers to these questions is a basis for how you should appear and act as a manager.

I am not recommending that you be phony, nor am I telling you to try to compete for miss or mister congeniality. I am saying you should talk to your people and ask them what they need and want from you. Here are some things I believe employees like and dislike.

Employees crave respect – Often, employees feel their managers don't respect their ability, their thinking, and their personal lives. I believe managers should go out of their way to show due respect to each employee in the organization and especially in their team. Respect is reciprocal: if you show respect to your employees, they will show respect for you.

Employees hate micromanagers and under-performing managers – Repeat after me: managers should never smother people and breathe down their necks all day and every day! In short: if your employees are good workers, don't micromanage. Just step back and let them do their thing.

However, avoid the opposite of micromanagement—under-management. Employees have needs and concerns both emotionally and materially. Under-managed employees receive little or no support, which leads to resentment as well as apathy.

Employees tend to dislike meetings and too much information (TMI)—Meetings are a necessary evil, but usually end up being a mad exchange of information, rarely leading to higher-level thinking. Limit the amount of time employees spend in meetings and find better ways of getting their thoughts on what you should know.

Employees need to feel appreciated — When hard work (and creativity) is unappreciated, or unrewarded, employees will be resentful. In turn, resentment can lead to apathy. This is why it is crucial for managers to show they appreciate the work being done.

To conclude, let me say, of course, that all of my advice is easier said than done. You may not become "best friends" with your employees – some management writers say you should not, anyway – but you can treat them like adults, responsible thinkers, and contributing team members. This will gain you the closeness you crave.

Dear Dave,

I manage a younger group of employees. One thing I see is almost everyone is out for themselves and most of them have a sense of entitlement, where they believe things should just be handed to them because they show up for work. What can I do to make these people understand it is they who are fortunate to have a job and there is no room for entitlement or feelings of superiority?

R

Dear R,

This is a complicated question. Let me first say that different generations have different values. The way we (older workers) were taught to work, obey authority, or even work in teams is far different from the younger generations of today.

I am not going to go into rants about Generation X does this, or Generation Y does this, nor even take shots at the beliefs, behaviors, and attitudes of "Millennials," but I will say that the way we were raised and what we experienced is most certainly going to have impact on the way we work and what we expect at work.

Imagine if you will that management had to treat every employee as a selfish "maximizer of personal satisfactions" and workers who expect things to be handed to them without having to reach outside their self-serving comfort zones. That's entitlement.

Workplace Nomads

Some management theorists believe that human beings are fundamentally selfish by nature. Worse, our obsession with the "bottom line" has created an environment where workers believe it does not matter how we get to a profitable bottom line; what matters only is getting there.

I recall when I was a young salesperson in Southern Minnesota: my boss told me, "Conrad, I don't care how you do it, just do it!" Writing this makes me realize that I was being given permission – I was entitled – to be self-serving, possibly unethical, and given the green light to be what I had to be and just go out there and take what was mine in the name of "the good of the company."

The "top line" measures of people, processes, a cohesive culture, team work, sustainable innovation and quality can give way to a mad rush of "me versus thee" and the organization owes me something thinking. Also, we carefully measure our work and what we put out, because God help us, that is all we will and can do.

Rooting out entitlement and creating a performance culture that includes "pay for performance" takes a unified and sustained effort by management and a clear understanding by workers that you will be paid and keep your job if you do more than "just do enough to get by."

Management Musts

Managers must create incentives that align each individual's behavior with the goals of the firm. Here are several ways to foster the kind of environment where employees will want to pull together instead of fend for themselves:

Praise team accomplishments as much as individual accomplishments. When employees do things that help their coworkers, give them high praise.

Make sure bonuses reflect individual and team performance. Compensation, especially bonuses, must contain some meaningful component of achieving team goals.

Model and reinforce the importance of helping others – this sends clear signals to everyone that you value employees' willingness to look outside themselves.

Excellence must be excellent – do not water down what excellent performance is and what excellent achievements are. Mediocre is not excellence!

You can tell people to play nice and cooperate, but unless you take deliberate action to prove you mean it, many will resort only to what's in their personal best interest.

Dear Dave:

My problem is me. I just can't let go and feel I must smother everybody and every little piece of work to such an extent that it is eating me up. I don't know why I can't trust people to get things done and why I am such a "control freak." Even when I get home at night, I feel like I need to call people up at their homes to check on trivial little things that are probably OK. Help!

Signed: Controller

Dear Controller:

I always say that admitting you have a problem is the first stage of recovery. I don't have a magical 12-step program for you, but there is help for your "S-Mothering" compulsion.

Sadly, the management world is full of people who think manipulating (micro-managing) every little facet of employee work and breathing down people's throats is actually "good management." How can I put this...? WRONG! A Harvard Business Review article offers advice for micromanagers:

1. Don't lose sight of the big picture. The classic micromanager tends to zero in on details right away so that even the best work is nitpicked.

2. Avoid the need to make abrupt corrections, especially when you have given people work to do. Do not prematurely yank work back from an employee to clean up details.

3. When you can't delegate whole tasks, delegate micro-decisions. Everyone knows that micromanagers have trouble delegating, so at least allow employees to make small decisions.

4. Recognize the Golden Rule of management. Micromanagement is often the result of impatience and mistrust. Think about how you would like to be managed if you were the employee.

If life is a matter of making good choices, I think you know the choice you must make.

Dear Dave,

I am a Baby Boomer with not too many years left before I retire. I feel like I have seen it all and one thing that always upsets me is when new (young) managers come onboard and they have no idea how to treat older workers. We older workers feel like younger managers think we are from different planets. I hope you have something to say to these managers.

Old, But Still Kicking

Dear Kicking,

I've always had great respect for older people and I still do – especially because... I'm old! I recall when I was a young manager, I made up my mind to show respect to the several older employees I had. I made sure to listen to them, let them "play the teacher" and I showed a deep interest in what they do and what they have accomplished.

"Younger managers need to be aware of the age-based cultural differences and speak to them," said Robert Norton, an IT infrastructure consultant. He believes the "Jolt-drinking, futon-sleeping crowd" sometimes doesn't understand why everybody who works for them doesn't exhibit the same high energy and excitement about their careers and future.

Managers must realize older workers have a family life, or they're simply tired of working 70 or 80 hours a week. Maintaining enthusiasm as you become older gets harder.

Managers must get rid of their stereotypes and know older workers are individuals just like everyone else in your group. They have seen a lot, so learn from this experience.

Dear Dave,

I am a new manager. Some of my fellow managers tell me I should never get too close to my employees, because they will take advantage of me. Then, others tell me that thinking is bogus, because if you get close to your employees, they will do anything for you. What is the answer?

M,

Dear M,

Traditionally, managers were thought of as being above the staff and they didn't get involved with any sort of personal matters, or even try to connect with employees. They were meant to supervise as managers and employees were to do as they were instructed. There really wasn't much of a manager-employee relationship.

I was just talking about this issue with a friend of mine, who is a manager in southeastern Minnesota. We concluded that you can be close to your people and still maintain professional boundaries. Employees are not robots and they are people with sensitivities and crave relationships.

I'm not saying that you should be drinking buddies with your employees, but you can certainly be close enough that they will trust you when they have problems (and ideas) and also come to you when they have good news to share.

Relationship Research

One recent study asked employees who would be on their "people we enjoy being with" list. Clients and customers were third from the bottom; coworkers were second to last, followed by bosses, who were dead last. *Interacting with the boss was also rated, on average, as being less enjoyable than cleaning the house.*

Gallup Research found that employees who have close relationships with their boss are more than twice as likely to be satisfied and fulfilled at work as compared to those who do not. The best managers are not only experts in their work role—they are experts in the lives of their employees, which increases engagement and productivity at work.

What I have found is that many managers fear getting too close to their employees, because they believe it may be a sign of weakness, and because they think the employees will "walk all over them." Though, the popular and recent leadership literature states that manager-employee relationships are crucial.

For You

Great managers care about each of their employees as a real human being, not just a means to an end. Employees appreciate it when their manager stops by to see how they are doing, or they enjoy knowing their boss sincerely cares about their family and is interested in them.

A warning: When employees see a manager being "best friend" with a fellow employee, it may create an unbalanced work environment. They fear favoritism is happening, and think "select" employees are getting special treatment. My recommendation is to find "closest" friends that aren't employees, though some folks will not agree with me.

Also, what happens when a manager's "best friend" becomes their employee? How hard is it to fire your best friend? It must be understood that this best friend is your employee and they cannot be treated any different from all employees.

So, where should you draw the line and be friendly, but not best friends? Some say you should not socialize with your employees, such as hitting the bars or playing cards every week. I say you can be friends, but you must have a crucial conversation with them making it clear you are the boss, work must get done, and you may have to do and say things that they may not always like.

Dear Dave,

I have 16 employees reporting to me. Many of them do great work and I am proud of them. But, there are some that don't seem to care about their work or do just enough to get by. Their work is not bad enough that I can just fire them. Why do some workers take pride in their job and some could care less? Is it money, me, the times we live in, or what?

Signed: Manager

Dear Manager,

In his book, *Good to Great*, Jim Collins advises managers to hire the best and brightest, and make sure they are doing what they should be doing. He calls it, "Putting the right people in the right seats on the bus." I always tell my students: If you want motivated workers, make sure you hire the right people in the first place! Check out your job candidates thoroughly, interview the pejeepers out of them, and find out what turns them on.

Now, what do you do if you already have unmotivated workers in place that you either inherited or erroneously selected? Well, you could just fire them for not performing, or you can help develop them through training and motivation. I vote for option two, because I hate to see people fail and I hate it more if we, as managers, feel like we failed people by not doing all we could to help them. However, do not feel shame when employees fail themselves.

The American Management Association noted a number of motivational "hot buttons." Workers:

- o Find enjoyment in the work itself
- o Have a desire for a "piece of the action," such as sharing visions, missions, leadership, authority, and responsibility
- o Take pride in performing excellently
- o Have a deep and abiding belief in the importance of the work they are doing
- o Enjoy the excitement and pleasure of a challenge
- o Desire to exceed their previous level of job performance (being self-competitive).

Bateman and Snell, write that managers can motivate workers by:

- o Reviewing employees and their work to help them become more effective.
- o Offering appropriate and timely praise and recognition.
- o Helping employees see how their work is vital to team and organizational performance.
- o Training and education employees to become the best they can be.
- o Challenge employees and give them a sense of control over their work.

236

Remember that employees have a whole assortment of emotional baggage they bring with them including bad experiences and fears. They may have come from a company or department in which managers treated them poorly, or they may have had a job that in no way utilized their talents and true abilities. Their self-esteem may be low and they may be mistrusting of management in general.

Deeply probe job candidate's perceptions of motivation and find out what turns them on by asking:

13. What things inspire you and motivate you?

14. How do you motivate others? Do you? Do you care?

15. What things decrease your motivation?

16. If you could design a company that cares about motivating their employees, what would it look like, and how would people be treated and feel?

Listen carefully to what they say and do not say. Also, spend time questioning your present employees and ask them these same questions. You may get "canned" responses from them, because they may wonder what you are doing. Be sincere and emphasize that you believe in motivation and satisfying employee motivation needs, and you want to make the place a more enjoyable, productive place to work.

Dear Dave,

I am a new manager for a large company. Our problem is that everything is a crisis and we really never solve anything – just do Band-Aid fixes. Why are some companies always doing panicky "fire-fighting" instead of planning for the future and really taking care of problems?

R

Dear R,

Not all companies operate under the "Oh my God, we are all going to die" mentality. I am aware of many companies that practice providing "whole" solutions for truly urgent problems. However, I also know of many that operate the same way you describe.

I suppose we could say that "if all you have is a hammer, then everything looks like a nail." This means that some managers choose to go from crisis to crisis, pounce on them, and never devise ways to prevent the various crises from happening in the first place.

I had one boss who thought that he had a very productive day every day by putting out fires all day long. He never once thought of delegating work to people, or move toward anything that resembles "problem prevention."

In that vein, there are many issues that may be afoot as to why managers do not prioritize the challenges before them, as well as prescribe and implement whole solutions. Most company problems result from some systemic error, whether people, process, or resource related. Good managers find the "leaks" and ensure they are doing more than sticking their finger in the crack in the dike.

A Word to Managers

Identify where, when, and how problems often occur and think about ways to address the most critical in a timely and complete manner. One prioritization tool is to create a four-square grid and write "important" and "not important" left to write across the top 2 squares and "urgent" and "not urgent" top to bottom on the left side of the four squares.

Obviously, the items falling into the "important and urgent" square are those that need quick attention. The other 3 squares will contain elements that are combinations of importance and urgency.

And also, please, please do not make your employees nervous wrecks by acting like everything is a crisis. I know that some things that come up are urgent and daunting, but many things can just be handled by cool heads assessing the causes and factors, and devising true, timely and, realistic remedies. I believe that is called Leadership.

For You

As a new manager, you are impressionable and will see many different management styles being applied to just about everything that happens to or in a company. Sadly, some managers ignore crucial situations and hope problems "will just go away." At the other extreme, some managers will pounce on a problem like a ravenous, stark-raving mad Robin on a misdirected June bug.

One thing we need to remember is that you tend to manage the way you are managed. I know this may make you feel quite threatened, but it is a fact and you must not resemble this bad management.

Today, when resources are thin and everyone wants to do more with less, there will be more and more problems occurring ranging from simple accounting errors, to full-blown maladies that may threaten the very livelihood of the company. How they are handled, when they are handled, and how much in control management acts during these times will dictate how secure employees feel about the company.

Chapter Twenty-One: Leadership

History is replete with examples of great leaders. However, the true competencies and characteristics of leaders of the past is again becoming a front-and-center topic, especially in the workplace. In business, we have folks like Jack Welch, Donald Trump, Warren Buffet, Oprah, and Bill Gates. In short, you have various personalities – from humble to boisterous and pompous – serving as role models of "how to get ahead."

I've never been much for loud-mouth leaders. I guess I look for intelligence, analytical and people skills, and the ability to stay calm under pressure. I have a laundry list of other attributes and traits for my leaders, but I will simply say that I agree with leadership writer, John Kotter, who says it's not what or who leaders are; it's what they do that counts.

Leadership Versus Management

Leadership theorist, Warren Bennis says, "Managers know how to do things right; leaders know the right things to do."

It's important to understand the difference between leaders and managers. Managers are task oriented – they focus on the job. They supervise and direct workflow for maximum efficiency; therefore they tend to be more concerned about the process, projects, procedures, and policies ... and the results, rather than about the employees and their individual needs.

Leaders, on the other hand, are relationship people. They are concerned not only about goals, but also about the people who are involved in the process. They must have a clear vision, must be able to effectively communicate that vision to others, and must have a strategy in mind for making that vision a reality. They must be able to motivate and energize people and create conviction and purpose in the minds of the employees.

Change is good and the landscape of the workplace changes from generation to generation. Today, employees are no longer content to go to work in complete anonymity, though they desire autonomy. Rather, they want to feel significant, stimulated and challenged, all while having fun and being engaged.

Effective leaders build a sense of community, belonging, purpose, and fortitude within the workplace. They hire and develop the right and best people, but they also improve productivity because employees are more willing to follow effective leaders than non-effective individuals. They create desire within individuals and do not use fear as a motivator.

You could argue with me that good managers don't need to be leaders and that good leaders don't need to be good managers. I don't believe that for a minute: this new economy is requiring that any person – who aspires to be an influential business person – be what I term "leader-manager," where you acquire and implement the skills of both roles. The folks who get this right will be light years ahead of the fray.

Let's visit some letters I received regarding leadership in the business landscape. See if you agree with my responses.

Dear Dave,

How can a shy person be a leader? My manager keeps asking me to think about becoming a manager and it scares me, because I will be expected to lead and motivate others. I am quiet and a bit shy. I may not be cut out for it. Is there hope for me?

K

Dear K,

Absolutely, there is hope! Shyness does not inhibit your potential to be a formidable leader—a shy leader can be as effective as an extrovert. There is no correlation between the necessity to be a gregarious extrovert and leadership effectiveness.

Research shows that pairing extroverted leaders with employees who take initiative, are more independent, and speak out can lead to conflict, while pairing the same type of employees with an introverted leader, can be more successful.

Leaders use both actions and words to get things done. Bossing others and bullying workers to get things done shows little concern for the employees. Shy persons do not normally become bosses, but many of them do become leaders. The bullies become toxic bosses.

Beyond Trump

The reason why we believe that leaders need to be outgoing and charismatic is that that's the ones that attract the most attention in the media, because they make good press. The truth is, introverts are more likely to listen to the ideas suggested by their employees, and also be more receptive to them.

Because we often equate assertive, outspoken, and dare I say, "brash" people with leadership, we've sometimes made those whose style is naturally quieter and less showy feel as if they aren't qualified to become leaders. As one manager tells me, he would much rather see someone with substance lead versus someone who just "talks a good game" as the leader.

Leadership is about building relationships and figuring out how to be of service to those who need help. Leaders are innovative and creative people and they grow by constantly seeking feedback and learning, constantly seeking out collaborators, constantly taking "smart" risks and developing a capacity for resilience and determination.

Remember, there are no perfect leaders! That's why good leaders are always trying to improve themselves through self-study, training, education, mentorship, making mistakes, and then learning from them. That's why there are a kazillion leadership books, workshops, and training programs.

I would bet anything your co-workers would rather be managed by someone who can truly motivate them and help them become what they want to become, rather than be preached to by an overly-charismatic loud mouth.

Your Challenge

Leadership success is based far more on your ability to build close relationships with employees under you than it is based on charisma. To grow, you should take courses in management and leadership skills—many colleges (such as Augsburg, ahem) teach these courses.

Improving your skills will give you confidence and provide you with resources to use when you are feeling shy or anxious. Join a Toastmasters International Group. Toastmasters teach techniques to overcome shyness and build confidence.

Use what you have been given, such as a caring personality, business skill, experience, and intellect. The more you learn about yourself and your behavior, the better leader you will become.

Know that shy or introverted people are often more introspective. They often have a better idea of their abilities, their flaws and their psychological makeup than those who compensate for their lack of leadership substance by being brash and overbearing.

Dear Dave,

I think respect must be earned. If an employee has reason to mistrust management, then how is that employee going to have sincere respect? Many managers at my company just seem to think that because they have that big

title the employees must give them respect. As far as I'm concerned all respect must be earned! Right?

P

Dear P,

I fully agree. Anyone's title does not earn nor guarantee instant respect. Today's employees have clear expectations of what they want from their leadership. And, if they get what they need, they'll respect their manager. If they don't get what they expect, they are resentful.

My belief is employees don't leave companies, they leave their managers because so many who carry the title "manager" lack the training, skills, and natural talent to be really good managers. Many managers carry forward the bad habits of the managers they learned from, without any realization of how much damage they inflict upon themselves, subordinates, customers, and their organization.

The Origin of Managers

Most managers are promoted from within with little, if any, preparation and often, even less confidence in their abilities. In many cases the manager is the person who was most proficient performing a particular job function with little or no attention given to their ability to communicate, lead, or think outside of their particular area of expertise.

One who is given the title of manager based solely on job performance might as well say to subordinates "Hey I'm not sure what I'm doing, so help me learn how to be a manager." However, that would be a sure sign of weakness, so to cover that weakness they usually try to exert control or follow someone else's rules for success that may include the very things that make for bad managers.

Waning loyalty is common in the modern workplace. Downsizing, reorganization, and other corporate (ahem) strategies have created employee cynicism. "Trust me" won't work anymore. Managers can only earn respect the old fashioned way – true leadership.

Most managers either come out swinging and aggressively try to control employees, or try to be everybody's friend and are insincerely sickening. I believe employees would rather have a controlling boss than someone who is unpredictable, phony, and tries too hard to pour on the syrup.

I Am Not an Animal

During the industrial ages, it was believed that employees did – more or less – automatically respect their bosses, but even then, it wasn't respect, it was control and those days *should be* long gone. In order to be effective, managers need to see the difference between deserving respect and earning it, because motivating someone has nothing to do with position and title, but rather how one behaves…period.

Managers must realize that their employees are individuals, not simply robots. They need to make an attempt to get to know individuals on a personal level. This may mean spending time "in the trenches" to build respect in the workplace.

Organizational culture varies from company to company, and even within a single company. There may be quirks found everywhere and it is vital that managers learn these unique quirks and the history behind them. This sends a message to employees that managers recognize them as people and respect their individuality.

Giving respect is the best way to earn respect in the workplace. Respect begets respect and trust begets trust. One of my colleagues tells me that if managers want employees to trust and respect them, they must trust and respect them first, and if managers try to control people, they will resist their very presence. Healthy productive people don't like to be constrained by someone who needs to exercise a false sense of power.

Managers—the next time you wonder why people aren't listening to you, ask yourself what you've done lately to engage them and listen. The belief that people should do something simply because "You're the boss and you said so," is just not enough. Also, it's simply amazing what true listening and thanking people will do.

Earning respect requires dedication to building long-lasting relationships that are fueled by trust. In the end, a respectful workplace is more enjoyable and more productive.

Dear Dave,

With all of the articles and stories regarding unethical practices in business, I am starting to believe that we have become a society that is not ethical and people will do anything necessary to get ahead. Thoughts?

Ethically Alarmed

Dear Alarmed,

I too have seen a migration from what could be defined as ethical and honest practices to a, "we will do it until we get caught" mentality. However, I am a hopeless optimist who believes that people innately want to do good and may have stumbled because of unusual pressures, bad habits, or learning from bad managers.

In short, if we let ourselves follow a pattern of corrupt thinking, we will become this thinking. It's a choice – we can choose the ethical route or add to a business environment that will forever lack trust in agreements and business management. People will choose to do business with people they trust. Fairness, equality, and honesty are traits we all admire, so we must practice these traits and insist them from others.

Dear Dave,

I am trying to prepare myself for promotion opportunities at my organization. I have a college degree, but I have only been working for less than two years. My problem is that I don't think I have leadership skills. I am not even sure what I should be working on to develop them, even though I have tried to learn from the many books. How can I learn leadership skills and which ones are most important for managers? I want to look like a leader to get promoted.

Puzzled

Dear Puzzled,

You ask a thoughtful question indeed. The ability to develop leadership skills – so sadly lacking in many organizations – will serve you well the rest of your life.

Research shows the skills most important for managers are leadership, team-building, and communication skills. A company will be strong if managers possess these skills.

Go back to school while you are working and get a graduate degree in business, such as an MBA from my favorite college (ahem), Augsburg, right here in Rochester. The leadership skills you must develop include:

- o Leadership communication strategies
- o Team development and relationship-building
- o Leadership style development
- o Vision articulation
- o Culture and climate development
- o Motivation skills (yours and others)
- o Talent selection and development
- o Decision-making and problem-solving

Employers like their leaders to possess passion, drive, interpersonal skills, and confidence. There are scads of other leadership strengths to develop, but if you can master the above, you will grow and be promoted. Also, get more involved in your organization beyond your job requirements!

Dear Dave,

At my company many people are out for themselves and only doing things that will benefit them, and not the company. I am a competitive person, but this is taking it too far. How can we understand what each of us wants should be something that can benefit the company? It's like we are constantly fighting each other for selfish recognition.

Concerned

Dear Concerned,

First, let me say that I believe respectful debate and varying perspectives are mandatory for organizational improvement. However, self-serving behaviors and unhealthy competition are not. Leaders must inspire creativity and organized dissention, while selling unity of purpose.

Carole Nicolaides, of Progressive Leadership, Inc. believes internal competition can destroy your organization. She writes, "Internal competition drives business results" has become a mantra of U.S. companies and has actually backfired reducing communications and causing information hoarding.

I believe that internal competition can become so damaging that it leads to isolation of information, loss of employees, and corporate disloyalty. The solution is to create a true "team" environment improving the "corporate good" through collaboration and sharing.

One business and information technology consultant in Southern Minnesota I know believes organizations need to provide employees what they expect of them in clear and certain terms. He says, "One way of accomplishing this is to require employees to include in their goals and objectives what they will accomplish to help achieve the organizational goals, both individually and collaboratively. This could provide the employee buy-in and accountability. The employees' goals and objective can then be part of periodic evaluation reviews to continue moving in the organization's direction, not just one person's direction."

Unfortunately, the reality is different, people are still getting compensated and evaluated based on factors that kill knowledge sharing and team synergy including:

- o individual contribution (employee of the month)
- o performance evaluations that give only a few people the highest evaluation simply because everyone can't have an "A"
- o forced distributions on merit such as if one employee within a department receives a raise then another cannot
- o contests between employees for various monetary and non-monetary prizes

Quality management guru, Deming, argued that relative performance evaluations and merit ratings breed internal completion, and cause leaders to label people as poor performers, even though their work is well within the range of high quality.

When employees are trying to "look out for only #1," how can we expect to produce knowledge sharing and organizational cooperation? Here are some management tips to overcome unhealthy internal competition:

1. Hire and reward employees based on their ability to work cooperatively to reach corporate goals.

2. Fire people who destroy united communication.

3. Focus people's attention on identifying opportunities rather than competing with one another.

4. Create new compensation measures based on team goals.

5. Promote employees who have a history of building collaborative and unified teams.

The bottom line is that internal competition can create rifts within teams. Companies must sell employees on the benefits of true knowledge sharing and collaboration.

Dear Dave,

I see a big difference between organizational "politics" and "leadership," but I'm not sure that I can articulate it very well. Do you have any thoughts on the differences between the two? Do you agree that "leadership" can and should be much more positive and much less manipulative than mere "politics?"

M

Dear M,

Great question. Within organizations, politics are inescapable. However, understanding an organization's political systems is absolutely essential for leadership. Those that understand the "political landscape" of their organization are able to use it to advance ideas and initiatives that are essential to the success of the organization.

Some define organizational politics as the self-serving and manipulative behavior of individuals and groups to promote their self-interests at the expense of others, and often even organizational goals as well. Others define organizational politics as the use of power, with power viewed as a means and energy to manage relationships.

Common to all definitions of leadership is the notion that leaders are individuals who, by their actions, facilitate the movement of a group of people toward a common or shared goal. This definition implies that leadership is an influence process, possibly transformational.

250

How organizational politics is related to leadership can be better understood from the fact that organizational leadership occurs in the context of groups, where followers are influenced by the leader to ensure their commitment and voluntary involvement towards targeted outcomes.

However, the reality is that leaders use political leverage available to them under different situations in order to promote the organizational interests — smart leaders know how to deal with the politics that exist and may be working for or against them.

The Business of Politics

First and foremost, we all use politics to our advantage. I see politics as an endeavor to obtain personal gain, including power, money, ego-stroking, resources, or – as one of my business colleagues tells me – "that's the way we get things done around here."

Those engaging in politics may use manipulation rather than motivation and often trade favors to get what they want. In that vein, politics often has a pretty negative connotation and conjures up visions of cigar-smoking thugs working out "private deals" in dimly-lit back rooms. To a large extent – and sadly – this is often true.

Leadership, on the other hand, has more of a team or communal gain in mind. It's helping people get what they need and fosters collaboration. It's motivation, both at an individual and a group level, and is essential to help understand what exactly what people need and the best way to help them achieve it.

Clearly, some politicians are also great leaders — and some very good politicians are miserable leaders, but excellent manipulators. In the end, both leadership and politics uses persuasion and influence to get things done.

We could say that politics involves exchanges and it is neither good nor bad. It's merely a means of getting what we want. I view networking as politics in motion and yet, no one would say that networking and "schmoozing" are conniving nor deceitful -just prudent.

Most people would tell you that things will not happen unless people are on board with whatever the issue is or whatever the purpose is. People need to be "sold" on the "what's in it for me" rationale or they say, "Nope, ain't going there." Could we say that politics is just smart psychology?

Dear Dave,

I need to vent about how my company almost totally ignores all of the talented women we have here. A few have management positions, but I know their ideas are not supported the same as the men. I admit that my company tries to make sure women are not harassed in any way, but the fact is the women just don't get the respect or consideration that the men do. This is probably true for many companies. Is there anything women can do about this uneven treatment and be taken more seriously?

S

Dear S,

The answer is, yes, there are things that will help. However, the men - especially in leadership - have to be convinced that maximizing the talent of women is not only fair and right; it is just good business, because good ideas are good ideas no matter who presents them.

Women start careers in business and other professions with the same level of intelligence, education, and commitment as men, but a breakdown often occurs because of stereotypes, bias, and ignorance.

What women can do:

Women can actively build the mindset to become more self-confident emphasizing positive emotions. Katharine Graham, the first female CEO of a Fortune 500 enterprise (the Washington Post Company), said, "To love what you do and feel that it matters — how could anything be more fun?" Thus, confidence is built through the overt expression of the love for the work and the conviction that one's contributions are purposeful and meaningful.

Being a *prudent* optimist — instead of what my wife calls, "the Eeyore (poor me) energy zapper." This frame of mind can be crucial to gaining attention and respect. If one appears pessimistic, this can lead to energy-depleting rumination and turns people off. I'm not saying you should run around the office in a clown suit with a bullhorn screaming Tony Robbins rants. It's just that using the "glass half full" mindset is better received than, "We're all going to die!"

Building networks is crucial. People with strong networks have the ability to figure out where to go to enlist the people and groups necessary to bring energy to ideas and projects. Studies show that men tend to build broader, shallower networks than women, who tend to build narrower, but deeper networks. This gives men a wider range of resources for gaining knowledge and opportunities.

It is important to understand that you must "give before you get." Women who promote *only* their own interests vigorously are often seen as aggressive, uncooperative, and selfish. It is wise to help others with their initiatives, which will lead to a form of reciprocity, where others will help you in return. Show respect and you will get it back. Another approach is to provide and ask for help on a regular basis from influential men in the organization — this builds relationships and allows the men to play the teacher, which they love to do.

Build a track record. Past, consistent performance speaks loudly. You will gain attention and support if you have demonstrated thoroughness, effectiveness, and completion in past initiatives and challenges.

Present a business case for your ideas. You can't just blurt out, "We need more advertising!" The response will – and should be – "Yea…and…why?" Provide evidence and support for your ideas and claims. Also, solid implementation plans solidify the deal. Talk about the elements, the features, the benefits, and how the idea could play out and be measured for success. Present a systemic, thought-out proposal.

Be respectfully direct. Being direct is a much better option than not. Being direct is being honest and showing integrity. Don't apologize profusely. Don't beat around the bush and do keep it short. And don't dress up your requests with flattery, which can come across as manipulation. You may need to say, "I've patiently heard you out, so please hear me out."

Finally, don't perpetuate the stereotypes and gender gap. I don't know why, but I have often heard women demean women as a whole, including stereotypes of blondes, women's emotions, or even that women can't be tough enough to take charge. This gender-based stereotyping can be devastating, potentially undermining women's capacity to lead.

Dear Dave,

My husband and I are debating whether or not women make better leaders than men. I say they do and you can imagine what he thinks. What do you think? Or, are you like my husband and will take the men's side?

K

Dear K,

First, let me say ... "You're killing me!" But, I am going to take a stab at this and, obviously, I will be bold enough – or stupid enough – to have my thoughts and findings printed in this book.

My risk is if I lean toward your husband's position, I will need someone to start my car each morning. And if I move toward your position, I will be lynched, be forced to take a Testosterone test, and be flogged in a "man cave" while having to watch a continuous film loop of "Spartacus."

To be an "avoidance wimp," let me state that I believe any person – no matter what gender they are – has the capacity to be an effective leader. Throughout history we have seen the marvelous leadership displayed by women including Mother Theresa, Clara Barton, and Catherine the Great. You'll notice I am staying non-political here – "thanka vera much!"

So, in a somewhat questionable attempt to be "objective," I will take the position of … it depends. Some "experts" claim (and these experts include men) that women have the advantage for being the best leaders, because they are best at forming relationships and consensus, and dealing more on an interpersonal level.

In opposition, other "experts" claim men make the best leaders (and this pack of experts includes women), because men are more dominant, decisive, and driven. I invite these experts to come to my home and witness firsthand the dismantling of this belief.

Why Women Rule

Who can deny that Oprah is a leader and has moved, inspired, and increased the positivity of so many people? Who can deny that business leaders including Carly Fiorina (past Hewlitt Packard CEO) and Mary Kay Asch have been instrumental in facing challenges that would rock the foundations of any leader?

Some researchers have found, in large part, that women make most of the financial decisions, start most of the new businesses, are penetrating senior ranks rapidly, and that women's leadership strengths are exceptionally well-aligned with new organizational effectiveness & value-added imperatives of modern economies.

Others claim women are better salespersons than men, consider people and human needs more when making decisions, and tend to be substantially superior at planning, organizing, and covering details.

Why Men Rule

I asked one of my female colleagues whether or not men really rule the planet and she said, "We just let them think they do." Why did I expect a response similar to that?

In defense of men as leaders, some experts believe men are less emotional and deal with purpose more than personalities. Others have found that men tend to be more objective and look at facts over feelings. Finally, findings suggest men are more prone to being overtly confrontational and lay things out in the open, so decisions can be made quickly and decisively.

In summary – and I have been thinking a great deal on how to end this response both diplomatically and prudently – I believe the answer to your question is that it does not matter what gender you are to be a great leader; what matters is your ability to assess the situation, the people, the tasks, and the implications and impact of a challenge and act with intelligence and determination. This ability is gender neutral.

Dear Dave

My boss was a military officer and his leadership style makes me feel like I am a new recruit at basic training. He is cold, somewhat terse, and generally barks orders at us. We have given up trying to warm up to this guy. Is a military model of leadership effective? I dislike this authority and discipline?

Drop and Give Me 40

Dear Drop,

I feel your pain. My first position in sales was under a former Army captain and he was as warm as Attila the Hun. I invited him to dinner at our house and he told me, he does not go to dinner at employees' homes, nor does he want to get "too close" to people, because he probably has to fire them. True story.

I interview and enroll many ex and current military people into our MBA program. I always kid them about the need for me to "de and re program" them. Sometimes they laugh and sometimes I feel like I need someone else to start my car later on.

In defense of military leadership training, there are so many positives and valuable aspects to the training, including, the prominence of values, purpose, mission, and pride. Also, interestingly, military leadership training serves as the foundation of current "best practice" leadership skills and theories.

Companies Embrace Military Leadership Style

Researchers at McKinsey and Company discovered that one highly effective route of leadership is demonstrated by the U.S. Marine Corps. The Marines' approach to motivation follows the "mission, values, and pride" (MVP) path, which some researchers say is practical and relevant for the business world.

A couple of other organizations that follow the MVP path are 3M and KFC. Other companies marry purpose, achievement, measurement, and rewards including: Process and Metric (Toyota), Entrepreneurial Spirit (BMC Software) Individual Achievement (Perot Systems), and Reward and Celebration (Mary Kay).

The Good

Military style leaders tell their employees what they want done and how they want it accomplished, without getting the advice of their followers. Some of the appropriate conditions to use it is when you have all the information to solve the problem, you are short on time, and your employees are well motivated.

The Bad

Some people tend to think of this style as a vehicle for yelling, using demeaning language, and leading by threats and abusing their power. This is not the authoritarian style, rather it is an abusive, unprofessional style called "bossing people around." It has no place in a leader's repertoire.

The Ugly

Some military-bred leaders act domineering and superior with people. They believe the only way to get things done is through penalties, such as loss of job, days off without pay, reprimanding employees in front of others, etc. They believe their authority is increased by "frightening everyone" into higher levels of productivity. Yet what always happens when this approach is used wrongly is that morale falls; which of course leads to lower productivity.

Finally ...

Leaders do not command excellence, they build excellence. Excellence is "being all you can be" within the bounds of doing what is right for your organization. To reach excellence you must first be a leader of good character and treat people like people, not robots!

Organizations will not achieve excellence by having leaders do whatever they have to in order to get the job done, and then hope their leaders acted with good character. This type of thinking is backwards.

Dear Dave,

I came to my current company without a lot of education and worked my way up. Our company tries to offer training opportunities and I am thankful for that. Lately, my boss is on a management training kick and we are getting trained to be better leaders and managers. I am confused. I thought managers were supposed to be leaders and that is why they got the job. What is the difference?

Signed: Unclear

258

Dear Unclear,

Leadership writer Warren Bennis wrote, "Managers know how to do things right, but leaders know the right things to do." In short, managers understand processes and how to get things done through people, and leaders know how to get people to go beyond just getting things done and stay motivated to do wonderful work.

Companies have learned they need leaders who can inspire, energize, build trust, and get people to follow a shared vision. While managers assume the more directive nature of work; they plan, organize, coordinate, and control things, leaders get people truly engaged and enthused.

Bennis also says, "Not all managers are good leaders and not all leaders are good managers." If a company can find strong managers that can lead well, I think they should hire them. Try to be one of those managers.

Dear Dave,

All I hear about at work is our core values and how these values shape and guide our company. From what I see, the only values being practiced are making money, working people to death, and doing anything and everything needed to do business. The core values we have written in our company statements, such as honesty, integrity, and collaboration are nowhere to be found. Maybe my values are too high for where I work.

R

Dear R,

You nailed it! What is written and what is enacted are often two different things when it comes to values and actual business practices.

Ethics writers say that companies have both espoused (written) values and practiced values. In short, you can talk a good game when it comes to values, but when it comes to behaving, these beliefs fly out the window.

I would venture to state that your company is experiencing the pressure to produce like everyone these days, and values seem to get in the way. It's just like "white lies:" how far can you stretch the truth before it resembles only a bogus, self-serving lie? Accordingly, some companies use "situational values," where values are upheld only if it is convenient.

Ethics Is the Heart of Leadership

What did we learn when we were young? Hopefully – depending on the neighborhood we grew up in and what kind of parents we had – we were taught to be caring, ethical, truthful, and obedient little creatures. Then, we are tested – and often tested harshly – and many throw their values out like yesterday's paper.

This trashing of values is amplified when people are thrown together in a corporate environment and the expectations of them are unusually demanding. Some company managers become weak and say they will wander from their values "just this once" (to address a situation) and they will never do it again. How's that working for them?.

Leaders must model the values and enforce them constantly. Leaders are watched closely by employees and if the leaders compromise their values, the employees will follow suit. As my old high school football coach always said, "You play the way you practice."

For You

Stay true to what you believe. Try your best to live the values you hold dear as well as those the company claims to embrace. It doesn't matter if you are a manager or an employee, values are values and they are the glue that holds a company together. You start telling lies and the lies will consume you.

260

Also, remind your coworkers of what is right or wrong, and what the company should expect to see. Some coworkers may tell you to take a flying leap, but you are doing the right thing and right is still right no matter how people want to muddy things up.

In meetings, in projects, or in everyday work dialogue, ask questions about the correctness, rightness, and fairness of choices and ways to handle things. However, you don't want to be seen as the "choir boy kill-joy" with your inquiry; rather you should try to come off as a reflective voice of reason.

Finally – and I always seem to end my columns with this advice – if you find that the stress of being associated with a company that treats values like a disposable razor ... get out! There are so many good companies out there that let good values drive the way they operate.

Ω

David Conrad, Ed.D.:

Dave is Assistant Professor of Business at Augsburg College and is Associate Director of the Augsburg MBA program, directing the program at the Rochester campus.

He is also an independent business consultant working with companies in the areas of sales and marketing, management, and leadership development.

Previously, he was the Minnesota Enrollment and Marketing Manager for Cardinal Stritch University. Prior to that, he was the Director of Continuing Education and The Leadership Institute for Winona State University in Rochester, Minnesota. Prior to that position, he taught business and management for four years at Winona State University, and served as adjunct at Augsburg College in Minneapolis, Concordia University in St. Paul, Viterbo University in LaCrosse, Wisconsin, Saint Mary's University of MN, and The University of Minnesota.

From 1975 though 2001, Dave was successful in sales, marketing, and sales and marketing management for public and private companies in the wine and spirits, industrial, and medical supply industries.

Dave has an Ed.D. in Leadership (organizational track) from Saint Mary's University of Minnesota, a Master's Degree in Management from Saint Mary's and a B.A. in Psychology and Sociology from Winona State University.

He has lived in Rochester since 1978 with his wife, Patricia, RN (36 years of wedded bliss) and has three grown-up(?) children. His passion is teaching and helping people and organizations develop and succeed.